LOVE IN THE FAST LANE: THRIVE IN YOUR RELATIONSHIP WITH ADHD

EFFECTIVE STRATEGIES TO SPARK POWERFUL COMMUNICATION, SHARPEN FOCUS, MASTER TIME MANAGEMENT, AND MAGNIFY CONNECTION

ABIGAIL SHEPARD

© Copyright 2024 - **All rights reserved.**

The content contained within this book may not be reproduced, duplicated or transmitted without direct written permission from the author or the publisher.

Under no circumstances will any blame or legal responsibility be held against the publisher, or author, for any damages, reparation, or monetary loss due to the information contained within this book, either directly or indirectly.

Legal Notice:

This book is copyright-protected. It is only for personal use. You cannot amend, distribute, sell, use, quote, or paraphrase any part or the content within this book without the consent of the author or publisher.

Disclaimer Notice:

Please note the information contained within this document is for educational and entertainment purposes only. All effort has been executed to present accurate, up-to-date, reliable, and complete information. No warranties of any kind are declared or implied. Readers acknowledge that the author is not engaged in the rendering of legal, financial, medical, or professional advice. The content within this book has been derived from various sources. Please consult a licensed professional before attempting any techniques outlined in this book.

By reading this document, the reader agrees that under no circumstances is the author responsible for any losses, direct or indirect, that are incurred as a result of the use of the information contained within this document, including, but not limited to, errors, omissions, or inaccuracies.

CONTENTS

Introduction   5

Part I
THE ADHD JOURNEY: DISCOVER YOURSELF

1. UNRAVELING ADHD   13
   - What Is ADHD?   14
   - ADHD in Men and Women   16
   - Debunking ADHD Myths and Misconceptions   18
   - Diagnosis and Treatment   21
   - ADHD on the Brighter Side   25
   - Simple Summary   26
   - Journaling for Self-Reflection   31

2. HARNESS YOUR ADHD SUPERPOWERS   33
   - Improve Focus   34
   - Enhance Working Memory   36
   - Gain Self-Control   39
   - Stimming   42
   - Identify Strengths   44
   - Mindfulness Meditation   45
   - Journaling for Personal Strengths   48

3. NAVIGATE THE EMOTIONAL RAPIDS   49
   - Emotional Dysregulation   50
   - Harness Emotional Regulation   52
   - Manage Stress   56
   - Cultivate Mindfulness   59
   - Quick Meditation for Stress Relief   61
   - Journaling for Self-Reflection   62

4. BUILD PILLARS OF SELF-WORTH   63
   - ADHD and Low Self-Esteem   64
   - Improve Self-Esteem   67
   - Self-Talk   69

Embrace Self-Acceptance	72
Positive Affirmations	74
Journaling for Self-Acceptance	75

5. MASTER THE CLOCK — 79
- What Is Time Blindness? — 80
- Master Time Management — 82
- Prioritization — 85
- To-Do List — 88
- Journaling for Self-Reflection — 90

Part II
TOGETHER IN THE FAST LANE–BUILD A THRIVING RELATIONSHIP

6. LOOK THROUGH THEIR LENS — 93
- Effects on the Partner with ADHD — 93
- Effects on the Partner without ADHD — 94
- How ADHD Affects Sex and Intimacy in a Relationship — 94
- The Perks of Dating Someone with ADHD — 95
- The Challenges of the Other Partner — 97
- Journaling for Self-Reflection — 100

7. BUILD BRIDGES OF COMMUNICATION — 103
- Communication Challenges — 104
- Improve Communication — 106
- Navigate Conflicts — 111
- Journaling for Conflict Resolution — 115

8. FIND BALANCE TOGETHER — 117
- Share Responsibilities — 117
- Communicate and Establish Boundaries — 122
- Maintain Individuality — 126
- Journaling to Create Healthy Boundaries — 128

9. INTIMATE LEVELS OF CONNECTION — 131
- Emotional Intimacy — 131
- Physical Intimacy and ADHD — 134
- Journaling for Self-Reflection — 136

Conclusion — 139
References — 141

INTRODUCTION

"We have to recognize that there cannot be relationships unless there is commitment, unless there is loyalty, unless there is love, patience, persistence."

— CORNEL WEST

So, you want to improve your relationship but feel clueless. Trust me, I've been in your shoes and know exactly what that feels like. In fact, nearly every person on this Earth has felt the same way as you do right now. Relationships have their ups and downs; it's part of human nature. Even the celebrity couples you see hugging and kissing in magazines and on TV have disagreements and mundane conversations. That's right: Megan Markle and Prince Harry also argue about who is unloading the dishwasher. Oh, the dreaded dishwasher duty!

When you have ADHD, love and everything that comes with it can be a little trickier. Unfortunately, no fairy grandmother can wave her magic wand and sprinkle the solution to disagreements on chores, responsibilities, and finances. There is also no five-minute fix for poor communication and a lack of trust or understanding. But there is a light at the end of this dark tunnel: one that involves love, loyalty, commitment, patience, and persistence.

Chances are that your ADHD brain has convinced you that you're destined to be alone. Having ADHD often means you can feel lonely amongst crowds of people. Your colleagues make fun of your symptoms while you forcibly laugh at your disorganization and poor focus. Your family struggles to understand why you can't keep the house tidy or stick to your commitments. Healthcare professionals shrug off your symptoms and opt to overload you with pills while your friends come and go; your emotional dysregulation tends to scare them off despite you trying your hardest to manage it.

Society has left you feeling alone in your struggle, and now you're questioning if anyone could ever truly understand you, particularly your partner. Your ADHD brain runs a million miles an hour, overwhelmed with thoughts, ideas, and creativity. When articulating your opinion and communicating your feelings and needs, it doesn't always come out as intended. It's as if you're trying to complete a maze blindfolded, repeating the same routes time and time again.

You probably feel as if you're also balancing the weight of the world on your shoulders. While others seemingly drift through life effortlessly, daily tasks feel grueling and pointless. You can muster up the motivation to write a to-do list and plan your day but still feel like time has slipped through your fingers. You could spend hours tackling the kitchen clutter but miss deadlines, family commitments, and parenting responsibilities. You want to be there for your partner and celebrate anniversaries, date nights, and personal wins, but how can you when you feel like you're drowning in household tasks, stress, and too many commitments?

Maintaining intimacy and a deep connection can be problematic. Some days, your emotions will be all over the place as you struggle to manage them. Impulsivity and decisions that may have required more thought can get the best of you. Promises, commitments, and important dates seem to slip your mind. Meanwhile, intimate moments can lack focus and seem like you're not present. The symptoms of ADHD combined can place immense stress on your relationship, leading to detachment and dissatisfaction.

First, I want you to know you are no longer alone in this journey. From here on out, I will be by your side, guiding you through the trials and triumphs of ADHD. No matter how difficult the situation, you can overcome it. With open and honest communication, support, and the right strategies in place, nothing is impossible.

Within the pages of this book, you will experience a transformative journey that will elevate your relationship with your partner and yourself. You will learn life-changing strategies that help you manage your symptoms of ADHD. You can forget the stress of reading through generic and subpar advice without a solid foundation. Instead, you will learn practical and effective techniques that have been tested and proven to work. You will gain insight from the latest scientific research and case studies, allowing you to trust that you will emerge strong and successful.

Both you and your partner will feel empowered to build a fulfilling partnership that celebrates your strengths rather than focuses on your challenges. Your communication will improve, conflict will be a thing of the past, and your emotional connection will deepen. Unlike other solutions, you will be offered a dual approach to your relationship, considering both you and your partner's needs, feelings, and situations. Finally, you will receive a tailored solution to often-overlooked struggles.

We will kick off this journey in Part 1 by focusing on you. Self-discovery will help you understand your emotions, values, needs, and boundaries. With your increased self-awareness, you will learn effective management strategies specifically designed for individuals with ADHD. This means that managing emotions, organizing time, engaging in the present moment, and communicating will become effortless practices. As you begin this journey of self-discovery, you will reconnect with your authentic self, loving, embracing, and accepting yourself for who you are.

In Part 2, our focus will shift to a more collaborative approach, where you and your partner will work together to apply these newfound skills in your relationship. Your empathy, connection, and communication will deepen as you focus on improving your understanding and creating a supportive environment. And, no—this won't be the same old generic advice you've been given time and time again. You will take a hands-on approach with actionable steps, real-life examples, and exercises designed to improve your relationship.

This journey will not be easy, but it will be worth it. As you navigate the relationship with yourself and your partner, the contents of this book will be your companion. Get ready to experience:

- Enhanced understanding and management of your ADHD symptoms
- Improved communication skills for expressing emotions and needs effectively
- Strategies for managing stress, overwhelm, and impulsivity

- Development of a deeper emotional connection with your partner
- Practical techniques for enhancing intimacy and strengthening your relationship
- Tailored solutions to address the unique challenges that you face
- Hands-on approach with actionable steps, real-life examples, and exercises for tangible progress and results

As we begin this transformative journey, I urge you to take the first step. Dive into the pages of this book with an open heart and a willingness to embrace change. By committing to this journey, you will witness your relationship blossom into a happier, healthier connection filled with understanding, acceptance, and fulfillment.

So, let's turn the page and begin. Self-discovery awaits you.

PART I
THE ADHD JOURNEY: DISCOVER YOURSELF

Many of us feel different because of our ADHD—almost like we are a misfit, the odd one out, or someone who doesn't belong. We spend so much time downplaying our strengths and focusing on our limitations that our beautiful attributes and traits get overlooked. It's time we changed this story and shone the light on positivity. Let's enter this new chapter of our lives with ambition, dedication, and optimism because you do belong right here, right now.

UNRAVELING ADHD

"People with ADHD often have a special feel for life, a way of seeing right into the heart of matters, while others have to reason their way methodically."

— DR. EDWARD M. HALLOWELL

Before we jump into exploring our relationships and working with our partners, we must spend some time strengthening our connection with ourselves. Once our mind and body work in harmony, we can begin directing our attention to other elements in our lives. Understanding your ADHD is the first step to developing life-long strategies; this chapter will allow you to gain insight into how your mind works and functions. In turn, you can adapt your daily routines, schedules, and habits, effectively creating a much healthier lifestyle for yourself.

WHAT IS ADHD?

Attention-deficit/hyperactivity disorder (ADHD) is one of the most common disorders to arise in childhood. This neurodevelopmental condition is characterized by brain differences that affect attention, behavior, and activity levels. There are three main types of ADHD:

- **Inattentive Type:** Just like its name suggests, the inattentive type of ADHD is when individuals struggle predominantly with maintaining their focus, staying on track, and keeping organized.
- **Hyperactive/Impulsive Type:** Hyperactivity and impulsivity often go hand in hand, leading to the individual struggling to sit still, finding it difficult to keep thoughts and opinions to themselves, having boundless energy, and excessively fidgeting. They may also make decisions without thinking them through or considering the potential consequences of their actions.
- **Combined Type:** Combined type is where someone experiences both inattentive and hyperactive/impulsive symptoms. They meet the criteria for both types of ADHD.

For a more detailed description of the types of ADHD, check out the summary boxes at the end of the chapter. A simplified list details the exact symptoms of each type of ADHD.

The ADHD brain is affected by a hormone and neurotransmitter known as norepinephrine. This chemical is similar to dopamine and influences your fight-or-flight reaction. According to research conducted by Silver (2017), an ADHD brain has significantly low levels of norepinephrine, which leads to the impairment of four different areas of the brain:

1. **Frontal Cortex:** This area of the brain controls most of your functioning, such as organization, executive function, and attention.
2. **Limbic System:** This area is hidden deep within your brain, managing your emotions and influencing your focus.
3. **Basal Ganglia:** The basal ganglia helps send messages and frequencies to all areas of the body. Symptoms like impulsivity and hyperactivity occur when these messages are interrupted or deficient.
4. **Reticular Activating System:** This system of nerve pathways connects to the spinal cord. Once again, once this system is interrupted or deficient, it creates symptoms of impulsivity, inattention, and hyperactivity.

The effects on these four areas of the brain are what set a neurotypical and neurodivergent mind apart. Let's take a closer look:

- **Functioning:** ADHD affects how the brain functions in different ways. It can change how you think, behave, and feel. People with ADHD may have trouble controlling their moods and emotions, and the connections between brain cells may not work as well. The brain has networks of nerve cells that send messages throughout. In ADHD, these networks may develop more slowly and work less effectively, affecting focus, movement, and feelings of reward.
- **Structure:** According to research from Hoogman et al. (2017), children with ADHD may have slightly smaller brains that take longer to mature compared to children without ADHD. Differences in brain volume are often found in regions like the amygdala and hippocampus,

which are linked to motivation, memory, and emotion management. The effects of this slow growth can impact cognitive functioning, such as attention, impulse control, and social behavior, up into adulthood. It's important to note that brain size doesn't impact intelligence!

ADHD IN MEN AND WOMEN

Have you ever wondered what differences exist between men and women with ADHD? Well, let's find out!

While ADHD can present itself differently in everyone, a few underlying traits and symptoms set the two genders apart. As a woman with ADHD, you bear the responsibility of having to conform to societal expectations, whether you realize it or not. This means that you could be struggling with feelings of inadequacy, overwhelm, and despair while also managing the pressure of supporting your family. You're supposed to be nurturing and kind, but you're dealing with deep feelings of anger, sadness, and guilt that can feel impossible to control. Relatives, friends, and even your partner may expect you to keep the house tidy, but how can you when you struggle to stay focused and your period, menopause, and fluctuating hormones are intensifying all of your symptoms of ADHD?

Women are less likely to externalize their ADHD symptoms; we keep them concealed and hidden within us. This is why that little voice in your head can't stop overthinking and criticizing your every move. If we break it down, we can see that women typically struggle with the following symptoms:

- Overwhelming feelings of despair, inadequacy, and stress
- Lack of motivation
- Disorganization, forgetfulness, and frequent tardiness

- Impatience
- Fatigue and trouble sleeping
- Difficulty maintaining focus, often accompanied by daydreams
- Struggles with eating habits
- Increased sexual desire
- A tendency toward body-focused repetitive behaviors like skin-picking or nail-biting
- Emotional outbursts, including crying spells and deep feelings of guilt and shame
- Social withdrawal due to anxiety and sensitivity
- Fluctuating hormone levels that intensify ADHD symptoms, particularly during menopause
- Perfectionism
- Trouble maintaining attention during conversations
- Co-existing conditions such as depression and anxiety that often overshadow ADHD symptoms
- Physiological manifestations of anxiety, such as headaches or nausea

On the other hand, men externalize the vast majority of their ADHD symptoms. This means that their intense emotions are typically externalized as frequent outbursts or temper tantrums. Much like women, men can also experience low self-esteem. However, this manifests differently; instead of feeling body conscience, picking their skin, or avoiding social interaction, men are more likely to be insensitive to other people's feelings, feel a strong need to be right all the time, and exhibit high levels of sarcasm, defensiveness, and anger. ADHD symptoms in men also include:

- Tendencies to interrupt others during conversations
- Hyperactivity (e.g., fidgeting)

- Aggressive behaviors
- High-risk behaviors (e.g., substance misuse, speeding, unhealthy sexual behaviors, excessive financial spending)
- Disruptive behavior
- Frequently misplaced or lost items

One of the most significant differences between men and women with ADHD is the diagnostic rate. In a study conducted by Mowlem et al. (2019), it was discovered that girls with ADHD might need to exhibit more emotional or behavioral issues to meet the complete diagnostic criteria for ADHD. Additionally, the study revealed that parents tend to underestimate the severity and impact of hyperactivity and impulsiveness in girls while overestimating these symptoms in boys.

Another study by Murray et al. (2018) observed that girls are more likely to experience a rise in ADHD symptoms during early adolescence compared to boys, who may show these symptoms starting from childhood. Consequently, doctors may be more inclined to exclude girls from ADHD diagnosis due to criteria related to the age of onset.

If we take a closer look at these two studies, we can see huge gaps and issues with the diagnostic criteria for ADHD. Women regularly experience gender-related biases that result in them being underdiagnosed and not receiving the treatment that they need and deserve. Regardless of age or gender, diagnosis and treatment are fundamental for healthy mental and physical well-being.

DEBUNKING ADHD MYTHS AND MISCONCEPTIONS

Have you ever been called lazy for not cleaning the house, tardy for missing a meeting, or rude for interrupting a conversation? Trust me, you're not alone. Many of us get a bad rep simply for having ADHD; it's unfair, unkind, and simply not true. With this being said, let's blast some hurtful myths and separate fact from fiction.

Myth #1: ADHD Isn't "Real," You're Just Lazy and Unmotivated

There is a common assumption that adults who have ADHD are just lazy. If you have trouble focusing, constantly fidget, interrupt others, and miss deadlines, you're "lazy." Wrong!

While ADHD may appear as a lack of effort or uninterest, there is a huge battle happening in our heads. We want to be successful and achieve our goals, but we have real difficulty in daily functioning. Yes, you heard me right, "real"—ADHD is a real disorder. Historians have even found textbooks dated back to the 1700s when ADHD was mentioned and described by Adam Weikard. Today, we have copious amounts of research and studies from psychologists such as Barkley (2015) and Roberts et al. (2015), who have dedicated their careers to proving that individuals with ADHD experience major life impairments.

Not to mention that Matthews et al. (2014) conducted a variety of brain scans between individuals with and without ADHD to provide tangible evidence that our brains develop differently. So, the next time anyone questions the validity of your ADHD, simply put forward the facts. After all, how could you argue with science?

Myth #2: People with ADHD Need to Try Harder

Telling people with ADHD to "just focus" is the same as telling a cat to speak English. In other words, it makes no sense, and there is no logic behind it. ADHD doesn't involve struggling to feel motivated or being lazy; rather, our brain runs a million miles an hour. Our brain is structured and functions differently from a neurotypical one, so our work and lifestyle habits can seem somewhat out of the ordinary. However, this only adds to the beauty of ADHD.

We often lack the credit we deserve. Finding out-of-the-box solutions and applying the creative methodology to nearly every element of our lives is truly spectacular.

Myth #3: ADHD Is a Childhood Disorder That You Can Outgrow

Studies tracking children diagnosed with ADHD over the long term reveal that ADHD is a condition that lasts throughout life. Recent follow-up research has also indicated that ADHD persists from childhood to adolescence in 50 to 80% of cases and into adulthood in 35 to 65% of cases (Owens et al., 2015). So, no, you cannot outgrow ADHD.

However, if you were diagnosed with ADHD as a child, you may have noticed your symptoms lessening or changing. Some people find that their hyperactivity or attention problems aren't as prevalent in adulthood as they were in childhood. Bear in mind that this completely depends on the individual and doesn't apply to all cases of ADHD.

Myth #4: ADHD Is a Learning Disability

While you may have struggled to keep track of work, deadlines, and assignments at school, this doesn't mean that ADHD is a learning disability. ADHD symptoms can get in the way of your work and school life; symptoms such as poor focus, fidgeting, and bad memory can play a huge role in your success. This is because you have *executive dysfunction*, those core characteristics you need to control your behavior, thoughts, and emotions.

It's also important to remember that conditions such as anxiety, depression, and even learning disabilities can co-exist with ADHD. This is one of the reasons it is so important that you receive an accurate diagnosis. With the right treatment, anything is possible.

Myth #5: Medication Will Cure ADHD

ADHD is a chronic condition; it can't be outgrown or cured. The purpose of medication is to help manage your symptoms so you can successfully carry out your day. Once again, this completely depends on the individuals. Many people with ADHD don't take medication for their symptoms as it doesn't agree with them. Hence, they take a holistic approach where strict routines, herbal remedies, and self-care are fundamental elements of their day. On the other hand, many people find medication to be incredibly beneficial. They can organize themselves, stay on track with work, and thrive in social settings. Medication cannot cure you, but it is a tool that can help you.

DIAGNOSIS AND TREATMENT

Receiving a diagnosis for any kind of medical condition can feel overwhelming, but that doesn't mean it has to be complicated. Let's break down the diagnosis process for ADHD to understand it better:

1. **Talk with Your Doctor:** The first step to receiving a diagnosis of ADHD is talking with your doctor. This involves explaining your symptoms, how they affect your day-to-day life, and when they first started to arise, for instance, in childhood. If your doctor believes you may have ADHD, you will be referred to a specialist.

2. **Formal Assessment with a Specialist:** This is where a qualified healthcare professional with experience with ADHD will conduct a physical examination to rule out the possibility of alternative health conditions. Then, they will ask you a series of questions; think of this as a little interview about your life with ADHD. They may also call a few friends and family members to interview them.
3. **Criteria:** Your doctor will examine your results and refer to the *Diagnostic and Statistical Manual of Mental Disorders, Fifth Edition (DSM-5)*. In some cases, if you demonstrate five or more symptoms of hyperactivity and five or more symptoms of impulsivity, they will diagnose you with ADHD. In other cases, a specialist may look at your previous school records and your childhood experience with ADHD. Then, they may evaluate if you have difficulty maintaining a job and relationships and engage in risky behavior. Check out the summary boxes at the end of the chapter for more information on diagnostic criteria for ADHD.

See, I told you receiving a diagnosis doesn't have to be complicated!

Medication

Five types of medications are typically used to help individuals with ADHD. Remember, ADHD is not a disorder that can be cured. Hence, these medicines aim to improve impulsivity, concentration, intense emotions, and learning. A doctor or health care professional prescribes these medications. From here, you will start on a low dosage and continuously work with them to monitor your progress and any adjustments that may need to be made. Let's take a closer look at these medicines:

- **Methylphenidate:** This is the most commonly prescribed medication for ADHD and is known as a stimulant. Stimulants increase the activity in certain parts of the brain that are responsible for managing attention and behavior.
- **Lisdexamfetamine:** Lisdexamfetamine is another stimulant; however, this type of medication targets impulsivity and poor focus. Think of it as a substitute for methylphenidate.
- **Dexamfetamine:** This medication is also a stimulant that helps reduce symptoms of impulsivity, hyperactivity, and poor focus. Methylphenidate, lisdexamfetamine, and dexamfetamine function similarly, but their side effects may vary depending on the person.
- **Atomoxetine:** Atomoxetine is a selective noradrenaline reuptake inhibitor (SNRI). This means it targets certain areas of the brain to produce more noradrenaline chemicals to help you manage your impulses and maintain focus. Typically, a doctor will prescribe you methylphenidate; if this doesn't agree with you, you will probably be advised to take atomoxetine.
- **Guanfacine:** This medication reduces blood pressure while enhancing focus. Once again, it is prescribed if stimulants such as methylphenidate and lisdexamfetamine disagree with you.

When taking medication, it is important that you pay close attention to how you feel, both physically and mentally. Stimulants such as methylphenidate, lisdexamfetamine, and dexamfetamine can cause side effects such as a loss of appetite, nausea, aggression, dizziness, diarrhea, and insomnia. Atomoxetine also has a high risk of increasing suicidal thoughts and depression. If you experience any of these side effects, seek medical advice immediately.

Therapy

Talking therapy is a form of holistic treatment for adults with ADHD. These therapy sessions involve discussing how ADHD affects one's life and mental and physical health and educating oneself on the disorder. From here, you will typically learn practical skills to set you up for success, such as improved time management and organizational skills, decreased impulsivity, increased ability to cope with failure, and heightened self-esteem. I know it almost sounds too good to be true, but it is all within your grasp. Below are two of the most common forms of talking therapy for ADHD:

- **Marriage and Family Therapy:** While counseling for marriage or family may feel like the last thing you and your partner want to do, it can be incredibly beneficial and help create healthy relationships. This therapy aims to help everyone involved; you will learn problem-solving skills and effective communication strategies and work on stress-provoking situations. For a family or couple with ADHD, this may be commitment, impulsivity, or intense emotions.
- **Cognitive Behavioral Therapy:** This form of counseling provides targeted guidance to develop behavior management skills and shift negative thought patterns toward positive ones. It supports people with ADHD in coping with various life challenges like those encountered in school, work, or relationships. Also, it addresses other mental health issues, such as depression or substance abuse. This can be helpful for individuals who have ADHD as well as a co-existing condition.

ADHD ON THE BRIGHTER SIDE

When it comes to ADHD, we often focus on the negatives rather than the positives. If you're anything like I was, there are a million and one things about yourself that you could pick apart. Maybe you suck at staying on track with laundry and household chores, you constantly forget important dates, or you misplace every pair of earrings, socks, and utility bills that enter your house.

This tendency to dwell on the negatives doesn't leave much room for all of your accomplishments, beautiful personality traits, and characteristics. In fact, I bet you've never given yourself the opportunity to consider your ADHD superpowers. Yes, that's right: You have an incredible skillset that can only be possessed by those with neurodivergent brains.

For example, hyper-focusing isn't something that anyone can do. It requires a skilled mind to intensely direct all of one's focus and attention to one task at a time. Now, think back to how many wonderful accomplishments and milestones you've achieved from your ability to hyper-focus. Perhaps you completed that huge essay in one night when it took others a couple of weeks. Maybe your deep concentration allowed you to harness your creativity and gain more enjoyment from a hobby or activity.

Creativity is another brilliant example of how ADHD can be rewarding. Aren't you thankful that you can think outside the box and come up with revolutionary ideas? Your brain hunts for unique solutions to every problem and creates innovative ideas that allow you to excel at work, on projects, and at home. A study by Cherry (2019) discovered that creativity goes hand in hand with curiosity. This means your brain is naturally ambitious, curious, and open to learning.

Bear in mind that if it weren't for your spontaneity and courage, you probably wouldn't be able to act upon this creativity. Our impulsivity can be a bit of a troublemaker; I'm sure I'm not the only one who has made a few too many impulse buys without looking at their account balance. However, impulsivity also allows for beautiful moments to peak through the darkness. Acting without fear or second-guessing yourself is something many people will never experience naturally. You can step outside of your comfort zone feeling self-assured and courageous, ready to make positive changes in your life.

Thanks to your thick skin, you have the resilience to face life's challenges head-on, even when they spike your emotions. Think back to when you failed an exam, messed up a work assignment, or let someone down. Did you run and hide? Did you prevent yourself from seeking positive change and improving your life? No, you didn't; otherwise, you wouldn't be here today. Your unwavering resilience has given you the power to find strength in your struggles.

So, the next time you feel low, beat yourself up, or just don't feel quite like yourself, remember what ADHD has given you: strength, courage, resilience, creativity, and spontaneity. These are just a few examples of how your superpowers shine in your daily life. Your ability to accept others for who they are and tackle every obstacle with enthusiasm and innovation is truly inspirational. Never forget that!

SIMPLE SUMMARY

Below are three simple summaries to help you understand ADHD more easily. Picture them as detailed maps to guide you through the complexities of ADHD!

Types of ADHD and Their Symptoms

Type of ADHD	Symptoms
Inattentive Type	- Struggles to pay attention to details and may make careless mistakes in school or work tasks - Has difficulty staying focused during lectures and conversations or when reading for long periods - Appears to not listen when spoken to, often seeming preoccupied - Has trouble following through on instructions and completing schoolwork, chores, or job duties; may start tasks but quickly lose focus - Experiences difficulties organizing tasks and work, such as poor time management, messy or disorganized work, and missing deadlines - Avoids or dislikes tasks that require sustained mental effort, such as preparing reports or completing forms - Frequently misplaces items needed for tasks or daily life, such as school papers, books, keys, wallet, cell phone, and eyeglasses - Easily gets distracted - Forgets to complete daily tasks, like chores and errands. Older teens and adults may forget to return phone calls, pay bills, and keep appointments

Hyperactive/Impulsive Type	• Fidgets with hands or feet or squirms in seat • Has trouble staying seated (in class or at work) • Struggles to engage in leisure activities quietly • Always seems to be moving quickly, as if driven by a motor • Talks excessively • Interrupts or finishes others' sentences prematurely • Has difficulty waiting for their turn, like in line • Interrupts or intrudes on others' activities or conversations, such as cutting into discussions or using others' belongings without permission. Older teens and adults may take control of what others are doing.
Combined Type	Experiences a mixture of both inattentive and hyperactive/impulsive symptoms.

ADHD in Men vs. Women

	Men	Women
Symptoms of ADHD	• Tendencies to interrupt others during conversations • Hyperactivity (e.g., fidgeting) • Aggressive behaviors	• Overwhelming feelings of despair, inadequacy, and stress • Lack of motivation • Disorganization, forgetfulness, and frequent tardiness

	Men	**Women**
Symptoms of ADHD	• High-risk behaviors (e.g., substance misuse, speeding, unhealthy sexual behaviors, or excessive financial spending) • Disruptive behavior • Frequently misplaced or lost items	• Impatience • Fatigue and trouble sleeping • Difficulty maintaining focus, with frequent daydreams • Struggles with eating habits • Increased sexual desire • A tendency toward body-focused repetitive behaviors like skin-picking or nail-biting • Emotional outbursts, including crying spells and deep feelings of guilt and shame • Social withdrawal due to anxiety and sensitivity • Fluctuating hormone levels that intensify ADHD symptoms, particularly during menopause • Perfectionism • Trouble maintaining attention during conversations

	Men	Women
Symptoms of ADHD		• Coexisting conditions such as depression and anxiety that often overshadow ADHD symptoms • Physiological manifestations of anxiety, such as headaches or nausea
How Do the Symptoms Present Themselves?	Externalized	Internalized
Average Age of Diagnosis	3 to 7 years old	Late 30s to early 40s

Diagnostic Criteria for ADHD

	Diagnostic Criteria
How Do I Know If I Need an Evaluation for ADHD?	• Difficulty maintaining steady employment, often changing jobs or quitting frequently • Struggles with academic or career success in the past • Trouble managing everyday tasks like household chores, bills, or organization • Relationship issues • Frequent forgetfulness or getting upset over small matters • Persistent stress and anxiety due to unmet goals and responsibilities • Long-term feelings of frustration, guilt, or self-blame

ADHD Presentation Characterized by Inattention	• Makes careless mistakes or overlooks details • Struggles to maintain focus • Appears not to listen • Has trouble following instructions • Faces challenges with organization • Avoids tasks needing sustained mental effort • Frequently loses items • Is easily distracted • Frequently forgets daily activities
ADHD Presentation Characterized by Hyperactivity and Impulsivity	• Fidgets with hands or feet or squirms in a chair • Struggles to remain seated • Experiences extreme restlessness • Finds it hard to engage in activities quietly • Acts as if constantly driven by a motor • Talks excessively • Blurts out answers prematurely • Difficulty waiting or taking turns • Interrupts or intrudes on others

JOURNALING FOR SELF-REFLECTION

Journaling is an easy tool for reframing your mindset. At the end of each chapter, we will reflect on the positive, allowing us to put our positivity into practice. With time, your newfound optimism will be reflected in all areas of your life. Enough chit-chat—grab your journal and pen, and let's get to it!

1. What activities were the most challenging for you to focus on in the past? Why do you think that is?
2. What are you proud of accomplishing recently, despite any difficulties you may have faced?
3. How have you been feeling lately? Have you noticed any patterns or triggers?
4. What are some things you'd like to achieve in the near future?
5. What activities or habits help you feel grounded and at ease? How can you prioritize self-care in your daily routine?

HARNESS YOUR ADHD SUPERPOWERS

"You can't change who you are, and you shouldn't be asked to."

— JONATHAN MOONEY

How many times has someone joked about your messiness? How often has a colleague or partner made a snarky comment about your tardiness? Can you recall how often you've been mocked for fidgeting, showing intense emotions, or having a "blabber mouth"?

Along with ADHD comes a lot of unwanted, hurtful criticism, so much so that it blocks out the light placed on our strengths. Now, you will take back the power and change the narrative. You will discover how your lack of focus can be channeled to enhance your creativity and productivity, leading to an incredible future. You will uncover the top tips and tricks to enhance your memory and relationship. Plus, you'll unlock the secret to gaining self-control and denying those pesky impulses that ruin your week. Together, we're shining the light on your superpowers and blocking out the negativity. After all, ADHD is an asset, not a burden.

IMPROVE FOCUS

When you have ADHD, your chances of concentrating are similar to a coin flip; on one side, you may be able to achieve everything you have planned with laser focus. On the other hand, it could take you a couple of hours to start on a simple task while your attention lingers between many assignments, chores, and thoughts.

This lack of focus can lead to a lot of people with ADHD ending up in what feels like a hopeless cycle. Tasks you don't particularly enjoy, such as work assignments, take a lot of time and drain your energy. Repetitive tasks like washing the dishes or doing laundry become so predictable that you just don't want to do them. Not to mention that learning a new skill or taking up a new hobby only lasts for a few short days; you soon find yourself jumping at the next exciting idea, leaving you a jack-of-all-trades but a master of none.

You're not alone in this struggle. In fact, a lack of focus is one of the most common symptoms of ADHD. New research, such as Sinfield (2017), has discovered that structural differences within particular areas of the ADHD brain play a key role in influencing our attention span. When combined with low dopamine levels (that feel-good hormone), our reward system becomes out of whack, leaving motivation, drive, and focus hard to muster.

Keep in mind that everyone's lack of focus can present itself differently. For some, it can involve experiencing brain fog, overlooking details, and making careless mistakes. For others, it may cause problems with listening during conversations, completing projects, and having to re-read information as their brain struggles to absorb it.

Whether you overlook the small details or are plagued by brain fog, the consequences of poor focus can affect both you and your partner. Typically, the person with ADHD will experience a decline in their mental health, creating feelings of anxiety, depression, and loneliness. As a result, this can take a toll on your relationship as you and your partner both feel your needs aren't being met. A lack of satisfaction ultimately means your relationship is being neglected.

Thankfully, you can implement various simple strategies to lessen distractions and enhance your mental health. Let's take a closer look:

- **Create a Thought Dump:** Do you know that feeling when so many thoughts are running through your mind that it makes it virtually impossible to focus? Well, a thought dump is a perfect solution, as it allows you a safe place to get all those pestering questions, ideas, and observations out. Invest in a notepad specifically for thought dumping. Then, when it is time to start work or complete a task, simply write a list of all your thoughts. Whether it's, "I need to put the laundry in the dryer" or "I wish the kids would stop having temper tantrums," this notepad will be the perfect place.
- **Interrupt Yourself:** Sometimes, we get so caught up in our thoughts that we lose track of what we should be doing. By setting frequent alarms for short five-minute breaks, you will interrupt your thought pattern. In turn, that sense of urgency you once had to complete the task will return, allowing you to complete the task at hand successfully.

- **Work Toward Clarity:** When you have a million thoughts in your head, it's important that you understand the task at hand; otherwise, it may become overbearing and lead to avoidance. If you're really stuck on a project, begin by asking yourself or anyone else involved some simple questions. Gathering details and information will allow you to create an outline.
- **Use Organization Tools:** As much as you may want to get everything done yourself, a little help from smartphone reminders, alarms, and calendars has never hurt anyone. Scheduling your day through apps and setting frequent alarms or reminders will help you stay on track with your daily tasks.
- **Use Healthy Distractions:** If you're going to be distracted, it may as well be healthy. Consider investing in fidget toys, stress balls, poppets, or even chewing gum. These simple and cost-effective distractions will give your ADHD brain the satisfaction it needs while you complete your tasks.

ENHANCE WORKING MEMORY

Have you ever had to re-read a page a few times because the information just wouldn't stick in your brain? Have you ever left a meeting questioning what you were told? What about doctors' appointments and anniversaries? Have you missed a few here and there? Chances are that if you have ADHD, you've experienced at least one of these situations. But don't worry, it's not your fault. You're not lazy, unfocused, or lacking motivation; your brain is just designed a little differently.

Many people with ADHD struggle with their working memory. In fact, a study conducted by Jones (2023) found that 80 to 85% of children with ADHD have problems with their memory, so it shouldn't come as a surprise that some of these issues have continued into adulthood.

Picture your working memory as a storage locker for all the information you take in throughout your day. All this information is held in your working memory until your brain processes and encodes it into useful or not-useful data. While your short-term memory holds this information, it also rearranges it, regularly updates it, and eliminates useless information. As you can see, a lot is happening at once!

While not everyone with ADHD has a poor working memory, it is a symptom that can be intensified by inattention, impulsivity, and hyperactivity. Remembering instructions, dates, and details can be tricky and potentially damage your academics, work, and relationships.

When you're in a committed relationship and struggle with your memory, you're typically cast as the "forgetful one," leaving your partner to pick up the slack and remember the tiniest details. While this may not appear damaging, it can affect your relationship in the following ways:

- **Conflict Avoidance:** I think we can all agree that no one wants to argue, especially when they can't remember why they're upset or what events led up to their feelings. However, avoiding conflict at all costs can do more damage than good. You have to take responsibility for your actions, whether your ADHD brain did or not.
- **Good Cop, Bad Cop:** If you're forgetful, you're probably also considered playful, spontaneous, and fun. Then, your partner has to come in and break the bad news, reminding you of daily responsibilities, finances, and reality. This system can feel unfair and hurtful toward your partner.

- **Judgment:** No one said having a poor working memory was easy, especially when you're judged and viewed as lazy, unorganized, and not loving enough.
- **No More Sharing:** After some time, your partner may stop confiding in you. They may view you as irresponsible or a grown-up child. This can be hurtful to both people in the relationship.

Luckily, there's a solution for everything, even poor working memory! To improve your relationship, academics, and work life, take a look at the following tips and tricks and consider implementing them:

- **Online Memory Tools:** Online memory games are a simple yet super effective tool for enhancing memory. Apps and websites that offer visual or verbal prompts and games can stimulate the parts of your brain that manage memory. Try aiming for games that engage your mind and focus; they should challenge you and require problem-solving.
- **Utilize Memory Strategies:** Finding the right calendar, diary, and organizational system can help you stay on track and remember important dates. Perhaps you need color-coded notepads, frequent reminders on your phone, or a big calendar in your office. Play around with different systems and see what works best for you.
- **Do One Task at a Time:** We know that our working memory is already juggling a lot at once, so we need to do as little as possible at once to make sure we don't forget anything. Instead of multitasking, try picking one task, setting the alarm, and focusing solely on that project. You could also use checklists with multiple steps to help keep you on track.

- **Exercise:** I know you've heard it a million times before and are probably sick of everyone telling you that exercise will solve all your problems, but I promise exercise can improve your memory. Research from Berwid and Halperin (2012) has even proven that regular physical activity can reduce your symptoms of ADHD and enhance brain functioning and structure.
- **Take Medication:** If you haven't yet considered taking medication for ADHD, talk with your doctor. Stimulants can help aid in memory function and decrease symptom intensity.

In addition, at the end of this chapter and in Chapter Three, we will discuss meditation, particularly a practice known as mindfulness. This is another holistic practice that works wonders for your memory.

GAIN SELF-CONTROL

According to The American Psychiatric Association, roughly 2.5% of Americans have ADHD (Parekh 2022). This means at least one percent are struggling with symptoms of hyperactivity and impulsivity. I know this may not seem like a huge statistic, but when you consider how disruptive a lack of self-control can be in someone's life, understanding the strategies to manage it becomes incredibly important.

Impulsivity can cause huge problems at work, school, and in friendships. Externalized symptoms of impulsivity can manifest in a variety of ways. Perhaps you lose control over your thoughts, opinions, and ideas and just have to blurt them out. Maybe you move around, fidget, and get distracted during meetings or in moments of stillness. You may even engage in unsafe behaviors like mixing substances, getting into fights, or recklessly spending all your money.

Keep in mind that impulsivity can look different in everyone. As we previously discussed, women internalize their symptoms more often than men. This may mean that her symptoms manifest in a more controlling, demanding manner, and she is quick to anger.

When you're a child with ADHD, teachers, friends, and family tend to overlook your disruptive behavior and cast you as a "naughty child." But, when you're an adult, you can't exactly blame it on naughtiness or youth. If you're anything like the old me, you end up being excluded from social circles, left out of work meetings, and no longer trusted by your partner.

Impulsivity can affect your relationship more than you may think. We're all guilty of stealing our partner's food from the fridge or watching an episode of a series without them, but impulsivity is more than that. It's chaotic: You proceed with your day, bottling up every emotion you have until one word or act from your partners tips you over the edge. Next thing you know, you're screaming, shouting, and crying at them over something that could have been solved with a simple discussion. As much as you don't want to hear it, lashing out can destroy the intimacy and connection in your relationship. It creates a stressful and anxious environment for your partner.

Impulsivity can also mean you often forget to think before speaking; you say hurtful things without realizing it. This is similar to how you also act without considering the consequences. We all deserve a treat from time to time, but recklessly spending money saved for bills, food, or future goals can strain the relationship. Once that money is gone, all you can do is wait for your next paycheck while your partner has to pick up the slack. In other words, it shows your partner that you didn't consider their feelings.

Self-control is incredibly important for a loving relationship and your safety. Making poor choices and taking unnecessary risks in the spur of the moment can potentially result in life-threatening situations. To ensure this doesn't happen, begin by implementing the following strategies below:

- **Understand How Your ADHD Functions:** ADHD manifests differently in everyone, which is why it's important to take the time to understand how yours functions. To start, try writing a list of what behaviors you consider impulsive in yourself, what behaviors others believe are impulsive in you, what recent impulsive actions you've taken, and what the consequences were. This will help you identify your principal impulsive behaviors.
- **Be Mindful:** While it may be easier said than done, checking back in with the present moment and allowing feelings to pass without judgment can reduce impulsivity. Mindfulness can also put some much-needed space between you and your impulses. At the end of this chapter, we'll take a closer look at how to practice mindfulness.
- **Stop the Action:** How often have you blurted out something and bit your tongue after the regret sank in? Personally, this has happened too often for me to keep track of! Being spontaneous and creative is one of your superpowers; you just need to know how to harness it correctly. This means stopping the action and thinking for a moment.
    - To do this, you start by identifying what situations trigger your impulsivity. Perhaps your boss at work

makes the worst of you come out, or maybe the kids at home nag and nag until you become a raging monster. Either way, write it down.
- Then, when the situation arises, think back to the list and take a deep breath. You know this is a triggering situation, so take your time and place a finger on your mouth if you need to. Picture your mouth having a little lock on it; until your impulsive urges have calmed down, the key simply cannot open it.
- Proceed to paraphrase what your boss, partner, or kids have told you. This can look like, "So, you would like me to complete the deadline by...?" or "You're asking me to...?" This clarifies the situation and allows you more time to think before speaking.

Remember, managing your impulsivity doesn't mean dimming your creativity or spontaneity; it implies that you take back control and harness your superpower.

STIMMING

ADHD stimming (self-stimulatory behavior) is when a certain environment or situation triggers you to repeat movements as a form of self-soothing. Usually, this behavior occurs unconsciously, so you may not even realize that you're zoning out, humming, or grinding your teeth. Let's take a closer look at the most common types of stimming for people with ADHD:

- **Visual:** This form of stimming involves finding comfort in watching repetitive movements or examining certain objects or patterns.

- **Auditory:** This type of stimming can involve listening to certain noises, sounds, and words.
- **Movement:** This form of stimming involves repetitive movements using hands, feet, or other body parts.
- **Taste/Smell:** This type of stimming can involve repeatedly tasting or smelling specific things
- **Tactile:** This form of stimming involves actions like exploring various textures, rubbing your hands together, or self-hugging.
- **Oral:** Oral stimming includes behaviors like chewing on objects, licking your lips, or biting your nails.
- **Mental:** This form of stimming entails repeating specific words or phrases internally. Common examples include counting down from ten, reciting the alphabet, or repeatedly uttering the same phrase.

While stimming isn't inherently bad, it can be seen as fidgeting by neurotypical individuals. For instance, picture yourself repeatedly tapping your foot on the ground during the meeting because stimming through movement calms your symptoms of ADHD. Your boss and colleagues may get distracted and view this as unprofessional, which could potentially damage your career. Let's take a look at a few ways we can manage stimming and avoid it affecting our relationships, friendships, and careers:

- **Organize a time and place.** Setting aside a specific place and time for stimming can help reduce stress and anxiety. This could be setting aside ten minutes each evening before bed to engage in stimming activities and unwind for a restful night's sleep.
- **Think outside the box.** Consider a few activities that would provide you with the same calming, stress-reducing benefits as stimming. Activities that don't involve

stimming, such as exercise and socializing, may be great alternatives.
- **Make it fun.** Consider using a sensory toy or tool for stimming. This will demonstrate to others that you're using an appropriate outlet for your stress and be less distracting.

IDENTIFY STRENGTHS

The better you know your natural talents, the more doors will open. That's right: By understanding yourself on a deeper level and discovering your strengths, you can create a beautiful future. You can harness the power of your abilities in your everyday life and sit back while watching your relationships, career, and personal goals blossom. Not to mention that it will lead to a life full of joy, passion, and potential!

With this being said, let's take a look at what actionable steps allow us to uncover our talents and gifts:

- **Reflect on past experiences.** Reflecting on your past may help you get to the root of the answer. Consider your accomplishments, no matter how big or small. Think about school, work, personal life, and even relationships. Then, try to find the link; ask yourself what all of these achievements have in common. Don't forget to write it down!
- **Ask friends and family.** Your friends and family know you best and can objectively assess your strengths. Their honesty will help you identify your strengths and weaknesses, leading you closer to discovering your skillset.

- **Analyze your goals.** Everyone has a goal, whether it's big or small. It's that thing that wakes you up in the morning and drives you to get out of bed. Take a moment to consider what skills and qualities you need to achieve this goal. By examining what actions to take to reach your goal, you can pinpoint the strengths that lie within you.
- **Practice self-awareness.** Practicing self-awareness simply suggests taking some time out for introspection. When you have a quiet moment to yourself, grab your notepad and pen and jot down your thoughts, feelings, and behaviors. Try asking thought-provoking questions, such as why you make certain decisions and how they make you feel. This offers the perfect opportunity to identify your personal strengths.
- **Accept constructive criticism.** While you may not always want to hear it, constructive criticism can increase your self-awareness. This will allow you to assess your strengths and consider any advice that could help you in your journey to self-improvement. Remember, this is *constructive*, meaning you have asked for the criticism and should be careful with how you respond; if the topic oversteps any personal boundaries, simply walk away and take a moment to gather your thoughts.

MINDFULNESS MEDITATION

As someone with ADHD, you may be thinking, *Seriously? Meditation? I can't sit still for that long; it's impossible and boring!* While meditation may feel as if it contradicts your human nature, it is actually incredibly beneficial for the ADHD brain.

Meditation is more than just sitting still and directing your focus to thin air—it's an intricate process that allows for the mind, body, and soul to connect profoundly. Becoming aware of the present moment creates a total and complete enhancement of your brain and body. Picture increased focus, relaxation, and impulse control as your stress, anger, and anxiety fade away. This is all within your grasp. Meditation engages your prefrontal cortex, an area of the brain that plays a huge role in impulse control, organization, focus, and stress levels. This means you are training your mind with each meditative session. Doesn't that sound incredible?

In Chapter Three, we'll take a deep dive into the intricacies of meditation. For now, try practicing the following two exercises:

Breathwork

We breathe up to 23,000 times a day, with each breath impacting both our thoughts and feelings. Hence, breathing properly is essential to a healthy mind and body. For this simple breathwork exercise, you find a comfortable seat and set your timer for however long you wish to practice. Then, follow these instructions:

1. When you're prepared, position one hand over your nose with your thumb over one nostril and your pointer finger over the other.
2. Gently press your thumb down on one nostril to close it off, and inhale slowly.
3. Once you've fully inhaled, pause, release your thumb, and softly close off the other nostril with your pointer finger.
4. Exhale through the open nostril, pause briefly, and then inhale through the same nostril.
5. Switch the nostril you're pinching again before exhaling.

6. Continue alternating in this pattern for as long as you desire.

Don't you feel better already? Breathwork helps boost your mood while enhancing relaxation and decreasing high blood pressure.

Body Scan

Body scanning offers an effective way to connect your mind and body. In the following steps, you'll discover how to engage with each part of your body, acknowledging sensations without judgment or worry. Find a comfortable seat and follow the steps below:

1. Start by softly closing your eyes and focusing on your feet. Notice any sensations, whether it's the texture of your socks, the firmness of your shoes, or the breeze on your toes.
2. Gradually shift your attention to your ankles, then your calves, and up to your thighs. Take your time as you move through each area, pausing to acknowledge the sensations without rushing. Are your ankles stiff? Do your calves feel tense? Can you sense a tingling in your leg?
3. If you encounter discomfort, pain, or tension, allow yourself to sit with it. Rather than avoiding discomfort, simply observe and accept the sensations as you continue to scan the rest of your body.
4. Once you've scanned your entire body, gently open your eyes.

Just like that, you have reduced your anxiety and stress with a relaxing and simple exercise. Get ready for a blissful night's sleep!

JOURNALING FOR PERSONAL STRENGTHS

Let's finish Chapter Two by grabbing our journal and pen to reflect on our personal strengths. The following questions will get that brilliant mind working hard:

1. What are three moments in your life when you felt exceptionally confident and capable?
2. Reflect on a time when you received positive feedback or recognition from others. What strengths do you think they were acknowledging?
3. Think about activities or tasks that energize you and make you feel fulfilled. What strengths do you bring to these activities?
4. Consider a challenging situation you successfully navigated. What personal qualities or strengths helped you overcome obstacles?
5. Imagine yourself as a character in a story. What character traits or strengths would you possess?

NAVIGATE THE EMOTIONAL RAPIDS

"Between stimulus and response, there is a space. In that space lies our freedom and power to choose our response. In our response lies our growth and freedom."

— VIKTOR E. FRANKL

Along with ADHD comes resilience and determination. You've overcome more challenges than anyone would believe, defied the odds, and changed the narrative. Now, it's time for you to separate yourself from the negativity. In this chapter, you'll learn how to use your strengths to your advantage. It's your moment to no longer be defined by your condition but be empowered by it. Let's embrace the positive and set out on a journey of growth and acceptance!

EMOTIONAL DYSREGULATION

If you've read anything about ADHD, there's a high possibility you've seen the word "emotional dysregulation" before. Emotional dysregulation is a mental health symptom that intensifies your emotions, making them harder to manage. It can significantly affect your behavior and may leave friends, family, and colleagues viewing your reactions as irrational or chaotic. This is because your reaction is typically disproportionate to the situation. For instance, picture your boss criticizing your work assignment and complaining about a few minor errors here and there. To your boss, this is constructive criticism that will improve your work ethic. But to you, this criticism can feel overbearing and defeat any hard work you've put into the project, leading to intense emotions and actions such as anger, crying, or anxiety.

Usually, you learn behavior management and emotional regulation as a child; it's a cornerstone to growing up. As you grow older, you become more adaptable and resilient. However, certain individuals with neurodivergence, trauma, or mental health conditions miss this step due to a difference in brain functioning. While others have a volume wheel that gradually intensifies their emotions, you have an on-and-off button that can go from zero to a hundred with a single flick of a switch.

Before you start beating yourself up for something that isn't within your control, let's take a few steps back and break down why emotional dysregulation occurs in ADHD brains:

1. **The Starting Point:** A small area in the middle of your brain called the "amygdala" handles emotional reactions and decision-making. Think of this as the starting point for all of your emotions.

2. **Message Sent to the Cerebral Cortex:** Your emotions are then sent to the cerebral cortex, which takes up 40% of your brain. Picture the amygdala sending a text to your brain saying, "Hey, I'm feeling really angry."
3. **Emotions Converted into Actions:** The cerebral cortex receives the message and decides what actions to take with all this anger. Typically, the appropriate response would be to take a deep breath and think before speaking. However, in an ADHD brain, the connection is weak, creating a reaction that is out of proportion to the emotion.

As you can see, emotional dysregulation is an innate process that happens to certain individuals. It isn't a lack of self-control or the result of poor parenting or poor manners. Emotional dysregulation can present itself in various ways; you may know it best as mood swings or unpredictability. Here are a few examples of the signs of emotional dysregulation:

- Self-harm
- High-risk sexual behaviors
- Severe depression
- Eating disorder
- Anxiety
- Extreme perfectionism
- Conflict in interpersonal relationships
- Suicidal thoughts or attempts
- High levels of shame and anger
- Excessive substance use

Someone with emotional dysregulation may experience damaging behaviors that are harmful not only to their own well-being but also to their relationship. Verbal outbursts such as screaming and crying, as well as aggression with objects, animals, and people, aren't considered socially acceptable behaviors; hence, emotional dysregulation can severely affect daily life, relationships, and careers.

Emotional dysregulation can manifest as jealousy, anger, and anxiety in relationships. It can affect your self-esteem, leaving you to question your partner's trust and love for you, thereby causing internal and external conflict. Intense emotions may mean that when you lose the TV remote, you feel like shouting at the next person you see, who happens to be your partner. A consistent cycle of intense emotions can be overwhelming for your partner, causing problems with intimacy and weakening your connection. Don't worry: Keep reading, and you'll find the perfect tips and tricks for harnessing emotional regulation!

HARNESS EMOTIONAL REGULATION

Emotional regulation is the opposite of emotional dysregulation; it is the ability to recognize and manage one's emotions constructively. However, emotional regulation is easier said than done. For many people, it is a skill that takes time and effort to learn. It involves a lot of trial and error and learning from mistakes in those fundamental years of adolescence and early adulthood.

Simply put, emotional regulation is the healthiest form of managing your emotions. Learning to experience intense feelings while responding appropriately can significantly benefit your mind and body. When we feel strong emotions like anger, sadness, and anxiety, we experience both a mental and physical response. While our mind processes emotions and reactions, our body produces a surplus of stress hormones, leading to an increased heart rate, spiked blood pressure, heightened temperatures, and shortness of breath. It doesn't sound great, does it? I think we can all confidently say that emotional regulation is essential for your well-being.

It's important to note that neurotypical individuals don't wake up one day and suddenly have the skill of emotional regulation. Rather, it's a conscious effort that both neurotypical and neurodivergent individuals must apply. The secret is understanding yourself better and increasing your awareness. Then, when something triggers you, such as your boss or partner's dirty socks on the floor, you can notice your emotional response. This allows you to consider the consequences of your actions and choose a response that moves toward a more positive outcome.

Emotional regulation is undoubtedly incredibly beneficial for your relationship. If you feel that your communication skills aren't the best, harnessing the power of emotional regulation will help you. It will allow you and your partner to communicate effectively without fear of impulsive reactions and emotions disproportionate to the situation. You will both finally be able to create a strong foundation for healthy and constructive communication.

Not only will tricky conversations become easier, but you'll also avoid unnecessary conflict. When you can effectively manage your emotions and view a situation for what it really is, those fights and squabbles about dirty laundry, drinks with friends, and misunderstandings become easier to approach and solve. The pair of you will be able to work through any and every issue!

Don't forget that a lack of conflict and great communication skills create more room for bonding time. Understanding your partner's perspective and thinking with a level head will allow them to feel seen and heard. As your emotional intimacy grows stronger, your relationship will blossom, and your bond will strengthen.

Now, all that's left is to figure out what strategies we need to implement to improve our emotional regulation. Let's take a look:

- **Learn Self-Monitoring:** Self-monitoring is one of the easiest yet most effective techniques for improving your emotional regulation. Observing yourself during neutral and emotional situations will help you identify and understand your emotions. Consider how you react and how long it takes for your emotions to intensify. You should also take into account what emotions you typically feel; try labeling them.
- **Tend to Your Physical Health:** You can't expect a healthy mind if your body lacks regular exercise, hydration, nutrition, and sleep. If you start prioritizing your basic needs and tending to your physical health, you'll notice long-term benefits in both your mind and body before you know it. Think about it; exercise releases feel-good hormones, while a good night's sleep and nutritious meals supply your brain and body with energy, effectively aiding in mood regulation.
- **Learn ADHD Skills and Coping Strategies:** According to research conducted by Lee (2021), a person's ability to regulate their emotions improves once their symptoms of ADHD are successfully managed. This means that by learning coping skills and strategies for your symptoms of ADHD, such as impulsivity, organization, and hyperactivity, your mood will reap the benefits and be far more manageable. If you think about it, this makes total sense, as our ADHD is often the root of our arguments, frustration, or sadness.
- **Stay Grounded:** When you're upset, it's easy to feel like the whole world is against you. You feel like everyone is judging you, past trauma pops up, and suddenly, you're

swept away with negativity. Grounding yourself will help you check back in with reality and focus on the present moment. Meditation is a great way to ground yourself, particularly by using the exercise below, "Fire Up the Five Senses."

- **Question Unhelpful Thoughts:** We all have an inner critic, that little voice in the back of our heads that likes to suggest unhelpful comments such as *What if they leave me because I'm too hard to be with?* or *I missed yet another deadline; I'm definitely getting fired tomorrow.* These thoughts manifest through anxiety and stress and do not reflect reality. Hence, it's important to question their authority and grounds for saying such things. Give others the benefit of the doubt and apply logic to unhelpful thoughts.
- **Add Uplifting Activities to Your Schedule:** When you live with ADHD, getting caught up in tasks you've forgotten to do and deadlines you've missed is easily done. However, this doesn't leave much room for enjoyment, meaning that we're constantly on the edge of erupting and losing our temper. Instead of allowing daily stressors to ruin your life, add at least one activity that brings joy to your day. That deadline is already overdue, and that pile of washing can wait until tomorrow. A relaxing bath, a walk outside, or some cookies with your favorite series will benefit your mental health tremendously!
- **Do the Opposite of Your First Impulse:** Your emotions are valid, and your thoughts deserve to be heard. However, when we're bawling our eyes out, crying, or burning from the inside with anger, we don't convey ourselves very well. For this reason, you should do the exact opposite of your impulses. If you feel like screaming at your partner for not taking the trash again, speak softly with them about the matter at hand. If your boss criticizes your project, and you

feel like bursting into tears, smile and say "thank you" for the constructive criticism. I know it's easier said than done, but sometimes, we must bite our tongue and push through to get a handle on our impulses. We can always return to the topic once we're calm to revisit the issue. You've got this!

MANAGE STRESS

Stress is the one thing we can't seem to escape. It follows us everywhere, whether it's work, family, or our love life. But how does this affect our ADHD brains?

Well, as you may already know, ADHD brains are typically under more stress. Every day, we face countless obstacles and hurdles in our path that increase our stress levels. When you're stressed, your body goes into action mode. This activates something called the HPA axis, which releases a bunch of hormones like cortisol that signal to your body that you're stressed. Picture this as your body's emergency response system to keep you safe when things get tough.

When this happens, your body shifts blood away from your stomach, as you'll probably not digest food while running from danger. Instead, it sends the blood to the muscles in your leg so you can run faster. It also redirects blood from the part of your brain that helps you think clearly and solve problems (not the time for deep thoughts—just focus on surviving!). So, when faced with big threats, the part of our brain that helps us plan ahead goes quiet, all so we can focus on getting through the immediate danger.

As someone with ADHD, your cortisol levels skyrocket when you're stressed; in fact, just thinking about a stressful situation can send your body into panic mode. This continuous cycle of experiencing stress and releasing stress hormones such as cortisol can be damaging to your mental and physical health. Your body is attempting to go through life while living in survival mode when there's no dangerous situation from which to escape. Over time, your working memory weakens, impulses become harder to control, and mental flexibility diminishes. Focusing will also feel virtually impossible.

Bear in mind that this is just the impact it has on you; we have yet to take into account how your relationship may be affected.

We previously discussed how those of us with ADHD tend to bottle up our emotions; however, when stress isn't dealt with, we end up projecting or even spreading the negativity. Both you and your partner will feed off each other's stressful energy, creating a chaotic and unsupportive environment. Until the stress is tended to, this harmful cycle continues. Think back to your last argument; chances are either you or your partner felt stressed, frazzled, or frustrated simply because they could see how much distress the other was in. You may have even said things simply in the heat of the moment.

It's essential that we find the key to managing our stress so it doesn't ruin our relationships and impact our health. Below are a few strategies to consider implementing for stress management:

- **Write Your Tasks:** Tracking all the chores, tasks, and assignments you need to complete will reduce stress significantly. After all, missing deadlines and falling behind on laundry, bills, and cleaning would make anyone feel stressed. Try keeping a daily to-do list with everything you need to achieve written down. Make sure it's realistic, and break big tasks down into small ones.

- **Add Key Events to Your Calendar:** We've all felt that dreaded feeling of "Not again, I can't believe I missed it." To help your working memory remember events, deadlines, and important dates, invest in a big calendar you can place on a wall you look at every day. While it may not be the prettiest thing to look at, it will reduce the panic and stress over missing key events.
- **Use Timers and Alarms:** Time blindness is real, especially for those of us with ADHD. We lose track of time and spend the whole day on one task while forgetting about the other assignments we have yet to complete. To help you manage your day and gauge the time better, set alarms and timers for however long you need to complete a task. Make sure this time frame is realistic and broken down; if you know a project will take you three hours, dedicate time slots of 30 minutes working and 10 minutes for breaks until the three hours have passed.
- **Try Body Doubling with Your Partner:** I'm not sure about you, but I spend at least 20 minutes of my day away with the fairies and my head in the clouds. If you struggle with daydreaming and staying present in the moment, having your partner be present as you both work on your own tasks can be helpful. Now, this doesn't mean they will babysit you; rather, they will motivate you to work harder and more effectively, allowing you to accomplish all of your tasks and reduce stress.
- **Set Financial Goals:** It's no secret that money is the root of many of our problems, which is why setting financial goals can help reduce stress. Financial goals will allow you and your partner to feel like you're taking financial accountability and working toward something as a team. These goals could include buying a house, creating a savings account for the kids, or paying off debt.

CULTIVATE MINDFULNESS

Mindfulness is a meditative practice that allows you to reconnect with the present moment and allow thoughts and feelings to pass without judgment. More often than not, we're swept away with our thoughts and emotions, almost as if we're caught up in a tide. They can feel overwhelming and dominate our day, leaving us powerless. With mindfulness, you'll no longer feel as if life isn't within your hands; you will regain the power over your mind and body, allowing you to process your feelings without criticizing yourself for being perfectly human.

Picture mindfulness as a tree with a variety of beautiful branches stemming from its trunk; these are different practices you can incorporate into daily mundane tasks. You won't have to worry about taking an hour out of your day to sit and hum; instead, you can cook, clean, or take a walk outside while engaging your senses, practicing breathwork, and observing your thoughts.

This alone will help you create a strong foundation for self-care and compassion. You will reduce stress, anxiety, and depression as your mind becomes as light as a feather. If you're wondering how meditation will help your ADHD, a study conducted by Basso et al. (2019) discovered that eight weeks of daily meditation successfully reduces negativity and anxiety while boosting attention and memory. In addition, research by Poissant et al. (2019) analyzed the effect of eight weeks of mindfulness training on a total of 25 ADHD brains. They found that it is a useful tool for relieving symptoms of ADHD and improving self-control and behavior.

With this being said, let's take a look at simple yet effective mindfulness techniques we can incorporate into our daily lives.

- **Practice Gratitude:** When we practice gratitude, we focus on the positive elements in our lives and direct our attention to the present moment. With regular practice, you will attract more positivity and find it easier to shift away from negativity. Just by writing down three things you're thankful for each night, you will wake up with a fresh mind and positive outlook. Plus, when you encounter a tricky situation, you'll be able to say, "Well, at least I have a healthy family and a loving partner to be thankful for."
- **Check in with Your Body:** Our busy lives tend to leave us without any time to check in with ourselves. Seriously, when was the last time you paused and thought about the sensations in your body? Take a moment to consider where your body is storing its tension, how heavy or light certain areas feel, and if you're experiencing discomfort. This will help deepen your mind and body connection.
- **Fire up Your Five Senses:** This is my favorite grounding exercise, as it allows you to check back in with the present moment after a stressful day. For this exercise, you will need to pause for a brief moment and reconnect with your environment. Start by engaging your nose. What can you smell in the air? Maybe it's freshly cut grass or lingering perfume. What about your eyes? What can you see? Perhaps kids are playing in the street, or the trees are rustling in the wind. Now, listen to what's around you; what can you hear? Are there people chatting or car engines revving? What can you feel without touching anything? Maybe your hands feel dry and rough. Lastly, what can you taste? Perhaps it's toothpaste or a meal you've finished eating.

- **Focus on Your Breath:** Breathwork combines mindfulness and breathing exercises, allowing you to alter your breath while consciously noticing your bodily sensations. If you want to alleviate some of the daily stress and anxiety weighing you down, this is the perfect meditation for you. You can find a breathwork exercise at the end of the previous chapter and a centering and breathwork practice below.

QUICK MEDITATION FOR STRESS RELIEF

It's time to get comfy and spend some much-needed time on our mental and emotional well-being. The following meditation truly can be practiced anywhere; however, for maximum benefits, it's best practiced in a relaxing and undisturbed environment. So, turn on your meditation music, pick out a few aromatherapy scents, and get to it!

Follow these instructions for stress relief:

1. Set a three-minute timer on your phone and find a comfortable seated position.
2. Close your eyes and take a moment to observe your current mental and physical state. Notice any thoughts racing through your mind or any persistent concerns.
3. Pay attention to your body. How does it feel? Are there any sensations of tension or relaxation? Notice if there are any areas of warmth, coldness, or tingling.
4. Shift your focus to your breath. Take deliberate, slow breaths, focusing on the sensation of air entering and leaving your lungs. Feel your chest rise and fall and your abdomen expand and contract.

5. Allow your entire body to engage in the breathing process. Notice how your shoulders, hands, and feet respond to each breath. Check in with your facial muscles—are they tense or relaxed?
6. Pay attention to your legs. Are they jittery with anxiety, or do you feel a sense of calm and stillness throughout your body? Try to merge with the rhythm of your breath and body.
7. When the three minutes are up, gently open your eyes and take a moment to reorient yourself. Notice any changes in your mental or physical state.
8. Resume your daily activities, carrying a sense of calm and centeredness with you. Feel free to repeat this exercise as often as needed to return to a serene state of mind.

JOURNALING FOR SELF-REFLECTION

The time has come again to grab our journals and trusty pens for self-reflection. Take your time and enjoy the process while answering the questions below:

1. How do you manage a challenging day?
2. Do you consider yourself more introverted or extroverted? How has this influenced your life?
3. What are some of your favorite life tips and tricks?
4. What are your thoughts and feelings about your current age?
5. If you could possess any superpower, what would it be?

BUILD PILLARS OF SELF-WORTH

"What we can or cannot do, what we consider possible or impossible, is rarely a function of our true capability. It's more likely a function of our beliefs about who we are."

— ANTHONY ROBBINS

Your only limit is your mind. Your belief system, life experience, and perception of yourself have created imaginary barriers, limiting you from seeking out your destiny. Think back to a time when you denied working on a huge new project at work because you didn't feel smart or capable enough. What about that day when you canceled plans with your friends because you felt low and hated your appearance?

The truth is, your ADHD has allowed you to be comfortable, stay in your little box, and not dare break the barriers. Chances are, as time passed, you progressively felt worse about yourself, your abilities, and even your self-worth. Now, that inner voice at the back of your head just won't shut up. Today, this all changes.

This chapter will be a huge turning point in your journey. Get ready to discover your authentic self and feel confident in your own skin. We'll learn life-changing strategies for building a strong sense of self-worth and self-esteem while blasting away negative beliefs. It's time to step out of your box and break free from your limitations.

ADHD AND LOW SELF-ESTEEM

As we work through this chapter, a few uncomfortable feelings, thoughts, and emotions will surface. Our self-esteem is intricately interwoven with our perceptions of ourselves; for someone with ADHD, this isn't always sunshine and rainbows.

When you hear the word "self-esteem," confidence comes to mind. Your brain begins to evaluate how assertive you are, whether you can make decisions with clarity, and whether you feel excited by new opportunities and adventures. What you may not know is that self-esteem also involves self-worth, including how much you like and value yourself, recognize your strengths, and move past mistakes without blaming yourself unfairly.

We all deserve happiness, love, and respect, but whether or not you believe it is completely up to the opinions and beliefs you've made about yourself. Keep in mind that self-esteem isn't something set in stone; it continuously fluctuates with everyone's individual mental health journey.

If you have ADHD, chances are your low self-esteem is wrapped up in a bundle of shame, creating identity struggles and a poor self-image. This is because neurodivergent individuals are usually blamed for simply being themselves. As they grow, learn, and adapt throughout their formative years, they may struggle with emotional regulation and experience frequent outbursts of anger, frustration, or sadness. I'm not sure about you, but I can recall a few too many times when I was blamed as a child for being "naughty" or "disruptive" because I had ADHD.

It's no secret that those of us with ADHD also have trouble with learning and may have to put in twice the effort to get the same result as someone without ADHD. This can majorly impact someone's perception and beliefs about their capabilities. Struggling to remain focused on a test or at work can leave you feeling like you're the odd one out, that you don't fit in or even belong. If this is combined with poor academic results or repeated missing assignments, the outcome isn't going to be positive.

Despite trying your hardest, you always face adversity, struggles, and hurdles, opening the door to low self-esteem, poor confidence, and a negative self-image. You may also experience issues with the following symptoms of poor self-esteem:

- Self-doubt
- Reliance on external factors
- Struggles with seeking help
- Anxiety and uncertainty
- Challenges accepting praise
- Negative comparison of oneself to others
- Critical inner dialogue
- Fear of not succeeding
- Pessimistic view of the future
- Undefined personal limits
- Over-accommodation of others

But how does this affect you now as an adult? While your self-esteem can affect your work life, it typically targets your relationships with others. In fact, your relationship with your partner can take a huge hit from low self-esteem. Take a look at its negative impact:

- **Failure to Communicate Your Needs:** Your low self-esteem has made you feel like a burden to your partner and everyone around you. Communicating your needs would suggest that you're bothering them even more, so your brain immediately turns on that alarm bell and stops you in your tracks. A great example of this is needing help with household chores because you feel unwell. You could ask your partner to lend you a hand, but you opt to do it yourself and feel worse or even hire help.
- **Sensitivity:** Has your partner ever asked for some space or alone time, and your heart immediately dropped into your stomach? While your partner simply needed some time alone, to you, this meant that you were unlovable and nearing a breakup. Low self-esteem can make us highly sensitive to feedback; whether a passing comment or simple request, the wrong sentence can send us spiraling.
- **Jealousy and Insecurity:** As we know, low self-esteem can often lead to a low sense of self-worth. Hence, our brain can come up with a million and one reasons why our partner deserves someone better, smarter, and more attractive, even if they're madly in love with you. This can also lead to an intense fear of abandonment.
- **Difficulty Being Yourself:** When you don't like or value yourself, you may attempt to portray a person you're not. This can look like laughing at jokes you don't find funny, agreeing when you disagree, and dressing in a way you believe is more attractive. Denying your true identity can

lead to further resentment and increase negative beliefs about your self-image. In turn, this enhances your insecurities, increases your sensitivity, and massively impacts your relationship.
- **Poor Relationship Choices:** Low self-esteem can lead to settling for less than you deserve. You ignore your core needs and abandon your standards as someone finally accepts you and is willing to be in a relationship with you. When things go wrong, you blame yourself and your ADHD and apologize profusely for something that probably wasn't your fault to begin with. This can create an unhealthy balance in relationships and lead to toxicity.

IMPROVE SELF-ESTEEM

It's easy to follow a few skincare rituals, run a warm bubble bath, or wear a cute outfit and call it confidence. However, making real improvements to your self-esteem begins by tackling the subject, understanding its importance, and implementing life-changing strategies.

A high sense of self-esteem doesn't mean you're perfect and never make mistakes; it actually signifies the contrary. A healthy self-esteem implies holding yourself in positive regard, allowing positivity to outweigh negativity, and accepting each mistake for what it is. It's a frame of mind where you celebrate your wins, find strength in the struggle, challenge your limitations, and flow through the ups and downs of life.

For instance, if you had a bad day at work or argued with your partner, poor self-esteem would tell you that you're worthless and the world is against you. With a high sense of self-esteem, you could move past the issue and accept any mistakes as part of human nature.

Considering the benefits of high self-esteem, I think it's fair to say we all desire to learn about simple and effective strategies to improve our confidence, self-image, and negative beliefs. Luckily, I have the perfect tips and tricks for you:

- **Believe in Yourself and Focus on Your Strengths:** An ADHD brain is practically hard-wired to think of the worst. This means that when it comes to getting stuck on a task or pushing your boundaries, you probably stand motionless, questioning if you're capable, considering your weakness, and believing that you are somehow defective. To combat this, take a small portion of your morning, three or maybe five minutes, to consider your strengths. Set your day up for success by reflecting on your superpowers. Not only will you feel great about yourself, but you will also confidently approach the day ahead.
- **Get Help Where and When You Need It:** Everyone needs help from time to time. Even the most intelligent, capable human beings require a shoulder to cry on or a helping hand. Whether you need a therapist, medication, support group, or a coach, getting help will take a massive weight off your shoulders. You'll feel seen and heard while getting the support you need.
- **Venture outside of Your Comfort Zone:** As I said before, our comfort zones keep us safe and relaxed. However, there's no growth in this; no one has ever achieved huge milestones by not pushing the boundaries and changing the narrative. Now, I'm not saying you need to try out for the next Olympics or come up with a groundbreaking invention, but you do need to step outside your comfort zone and learn something new. It will make you feel good about yourself and let you shake off some negativity.

- **Set Yourself up for Success with Mini-Goals:** Mini-goals will transform how you approach tasks; seriously, you'll thank me for this tip. Imagine you have a work assignment to complete; it requires a lot of effort and may take you a few days. Instead of writing down this big task on your to-do list, schedule every step of the project. Break it down into small parts that are easily achievable. You'll find yourself slowly ticking off the boxes and getting closer and closer to success. Before you know it, you will have achieved the assignment and gained a huge sense of accomplishment, boosting your confidence.
- **Ditch the Negative Self-Talk:** I can't be the only one who has made a mistake, told themselves they're stupid, and continued a cycle of self-hatred. In fact, I've probably even run out of insults to call myself! This is a common theme for people with ADHD. We enter a loop of negativity and find it hard to escape. The first step to combatting this is understanding that it's not your fault; ADHD is a neurological disorder. We'll take a closer look at this later on.

With these five simple strategies, you can boost your self-esteem in no time!

SELF-TALK

Do you ever find yourself calling your brain stupid or useless for being unable to complete a task? Have you ever beat yourself up over being lazy or unmotivated? Do you look in the mirror and call yourself hurtful insults like "gross"? Chances are, you do, and everybody else does, too.

Nearly everyone on this planet has an inner voice; at times, this inner voice is highly critical and negative and can punish you for simply being human. Personally, I like to call this voice your inner critic, a nagging sound in the back of your head that's pessimistic and judgmental. While this voice can be helpful and motivate us to achieve our goals, there are moments when your inner critic can take over and become detrimental to your well-being.

When this voice becomes excessive, you'll notice your mind entering a loop of negativity, almost like a dark hole that's hard to escape. You may feel hopeless and believe you're destined to be alone or defeated and give up trying. Perhaps you'll be mean to yourself and use abusive language or feel apathetic and slowly lose all interest in your goals. No matter how your inner critic manifests, it never results in a positive outcome. Take a moment to see how negative self-talk may be impacting your mental and physical well-being:

- **High Risk of Mental Health Issues:** A variety of studies have demonstrated how critical self-talk can cause depression, anxiety, post-traumatic stress disorder (PTSD), psychosis, and obsessive-compulsive disorder (OCD). This is primarily because negative self-talk leaves us feeling hopeless and decreases our motivation, causing issues with relationships, work, and an internal battle.
- **Increased Stress Levels:** Your stress levels increase immensely when your reality is distorted and based on a belief that you're no good or don't possess the abilities to achieve your goals. You begin to close yourself off from opportunities and give up on your dreams.
- **Perfectionism:** As your inner critic becomes louder and louder, it creates an unattainable idea of "perfect." This means that "great" becomes "bad," and nothing will ever

feel good enough. You pick apart the tiniest of details, no matter how well you've done on a project or handling a situation.
- **Relationship Struggles:** Our inner critic is our number one hater. Hence, it's probably convinced you that you're not good enough for your partner. Maybe your insecurities have even intensified, and you've become more needy and codependent. A constant need for reassurance can strain your relationship, just as much as sensitivity to playfulness can ruin the fun.

So, how do we get out of this rut and quiet down that annoying voice in the back of our heads? Let's find out:

- **Be Aware of It:** The first step to reframing your mindset is recognizing that you have an inner critic. This will allow you to notice when that pesky voice is speaking up and prevent it from going any further.
- **Name It:** One of my favorite ways to distance myself from my inner critic is by naming it. I know it may sound a bit odd, but giving your inner critic its own identity allows you to separate it from yourself and alleviate some of the blame. Try to give your inner critic a fun name, such as Nagging Nelly or Sour Sally. Mine is called Downer Debbie; she's a huge pessimist who puts me down for nearly everything I do!
- **Finish the Statement with "And" or "But":** When your inner critic chimes in on your day, don't allow it to get the last say. Finish every negative thought with "and" or but" to put a positive twist on the negativity. For example, if your inner critic says, "You're such a failure; you missed another assignment!" hit it back with, "But that's okay, I tried my best, and I can try again tomorrow!"

- **Use Positive Affirmations:** Positive affirmations are simple and catchy sentences that can be said out loud to reframe your mind. Think of them as mantras to help you in any and every situation where a bit of positivity and motivation is needed. They're also really helpful at combatting negative thoughts. At the end of this chapter, you'll find a list of 20 affirmations for you to integrate into your daily routine.
- **Be Your Own Friend:** You're going to spend your entire life with yourself, so why not be your own best friend? When a negative thought creeps into your head, question it and ask, "Would I say this to a friend, partner, or family member?" Chances are, you wouldn't, so you shouldn't be saying it to yourself. It's time to treat yourself with the same level of respect, generosity, and love that you give others.

EMBRACE SELF-ACCEPTANCE

Self-acceptance can feel confusing. What does it even mean to accept yourself, and why is it such a big deal? You probably think that you have already accepted yourself and that it's something ingrained in you. It's not like you walk around all day denying your existence. But what if self-acceptance is something completely different from what we believe it to be?

Self-acceptance means accepting every single inch of your body, each good and bad quality about yourself, without any hesitation, conditions, or exceptions. Embracing your positive attributes and skills isn't enough; you must love the ugly, negative, and undesirable parts of yourself. With self-acceptance, you embody your most authentic self.

I'm not going to lie to you and say this is easy. Self-acceptance can be extremely difficult for some people, especially if you possess qualities and traits that you're eager to change. But by accepting these ugly parts of ourselves, we can begin our journey toward improving them. Think about it; if we can't acknowledge these negative attributes and accept them for what they are, how would we ever be able to improve them? Skipping straight to the finish line and pretending you put in the work doesn't achieve anything.

Self-acceptance is essential if you desire to live a life where you share your most intimate thoughts and authentic self with your partner. You must first understand yourself to build a genuine connection without barriers or constraints. Recognizing the ugly, embracing it, and accepting your true nature will create a deep and trusting relationship between you and your partner.

Not to mention that you'll no longer fear the challenges life offers you. Knowing your limitations and weaknesses will allow you to harness them and use them to your advantage. Just imagine how resilient and determined you'll become to achieve your goals.

As I said before, cultivating self-acceptance won't be an easy task; for this reason, I've created straightforward strategies for you to integrate into your life seamlessly:

- **Be a Gentle Observer:** As someone with ADHD, your symptoms will be the most challenging part for you to accept. That's why we will start with a simple yet effective strategy that involves paying attention. Observe how your ADHD impacts your daily life, the good and the bad. With time, you will learn how to accept the ups and downs of ADHD.

- **Do the Work of Self-Love and Acceptance:** Self-love and self-acceptance won't magically happen, nor will they come with a click of your fingers. It is something that you will have to work at day in and day out. Don't just implement these strategies—live by them. Wake up and repeat your positive affirmations, continue to change the narrative each time your inner critic speaks up, and actively discover parts of yourself that deserve appreciation. Once you've gotten used to these strategies, you have to continue finding new ways to feel proud of yourself.
- **Educate Yourself and Others:** While it's not necessarily your job to teach others about ADHD, you must feel proud of who you are and what your ADHD brings to the table. Understanding the science behind your brain and how your symptoms influence every action is a great start. Now, it's up to you to decide your narrative; are you a victim of ADHD or blessed with skills, superpowers, and an innovative mindset that others simply can't obtain? Pave the path for kind and accurate interpretations of ADHD. It won't just help you treat yourself with love and acceptance; your friends and family will also catch on.

POSITIVE AFFIRMATIONS

As we know, positive affirmations are a super simple way for us to ditch toxic self-talk and quiet that pesky inner critic. Below are 20 positive affirmations to boost your journey toward self-acceptance. Find one that resonates with you, and speak the words into existence every day. Just watch how your frame of mind shifts from negative to positive!

1. I choose to respond, not just react, every day.
2. I'm progressing toward my goals step by step.
3. With each breath, I find peace and release my worries.
4. I trust myself to handle whatever comes my way.
5. There are multiple paths to success, and I'm finding mine.
6. I embrace my uniqueness as a chance to learn and grow.
7. I have the strength, honesty, and resilience to face any challenge.
8. I may not have reached my destination yet, but I'm on my way.
9. My values guide me toward a fulfilling life.
10. I focus on the next small step forward.
11. I am complete just as I am.
12. I am capable of making the changes I desire.
13. My mind is inventive and resourceful.
14. I can endure discomfort in pursuit of my goals.
15. I choose responses that align with my values.
16. Even if I don't see immediate results, my efforts will pay off.
17. A clear plan brings clarity to my mind.
18. I can handle whatever today throws at me.
19. One task at a time brings me closer to my goals.
20. My emotions are valid, and I honor them as part of my journey.

JOURNALING FOR SELF-ACCEPTANCE

Wow, this chapter truly has set us free from our limitations. Doesn't it feel great? Remember, your journey toward self-acceptance, confidence, and self-worth will be ongoing. You must decide who you want to be each day you wake up. You can revert back to your old self, someone who feels fragile and unsure of themselves. You can also take every lesson we have learned and push yourself every day to show up as the best possible version of yourself. That's what I choose; if you do, too, grab your journal and ask yourself the following questions:

1. What do I appreciate most about myself? Why?
2. What kinds of people uplift me the most in their presence? Who are they?
3. When was the last occasion I felt completely comfortable with myself? Describe the emotions experienced.
4. Are there moments when I manage to confront my fears? In what situations do I find it necessary to confront my fears directly? How do I approach this? Share a personal experience of overcoming fear.
5. What recent measures have I implemented to maintain a connection with my inner beauty?

BUILDING BRIDGES IN THE ADHD COMMUNITY

"In a gentle way, you can shake the world."

— MAHATMA GANDHI

I'd like to pause our journey for a moment to ask you to reflect on how you were feeling when you first came across this book. ADHD can leave you feeling terribly alone, especially if you've struggled with your relationships. Perhaps you came to this book with the hope of approaching your next relationship differently, or maybe you're in a relationship you're determined to protect and picked this book up in the hope of finding strategies to help you avoid repeating past mistakes. How are you feeling now? We're only halfway through our journey together, but I hope you're beginning to see how much hope there is for you in navigating a relationship with ADHD.

There are many other people like you out there, so despite how lonely it feels at times, you really aren't alone in your experiences. But I'm sure you've felt that you were, at least at times, so you understand that feeling that countless other people are struggling with. It's difficult to separate ourselves from our own experiences, and it can be hard to conceptualize that nearly every couple who seems perfect from the outside has their own struggles, regardless of whether or not they're also dealing with ADHD. It's true, though, that you have extra challenges to work with when it comes to relationships, and it's my hope that this book will give you the tools you need to overcome them.

I'd like to take this opportunity to call on your empathy for other people with ADHD and help me get this guidance to them too. That probably sounds like a tall order, but it's actually very simple: All you need to do to make a huge difference is leave a short review.

By leaving a review of this book on Amazon, you'll kill two birds with one stone, not only showing new readers that they're not alone, but also showing them exactly where they can find the guidance they need to make cultivating deep and meaningful relationships easier.

Reviews help people find the information they're looking for, and that little reminder that there's hope on the horizon can go a long way. In the space of the few minutes it will take you to share your thoughts, you could make a huge difference to someone else.

Thank you so much for your support. We're all stronger when we band together.

Scan the QR code below:

MASTER THE CLOCK

"Until you value yourself, you will not value your time. Until you value your time, you will not do anything with it."

— M. SCOTT PECK

As we near the end of Part 1, we can confidently say that we have unlocked our true identity and now understand the beauty of living life authentically. Before progressing into Part 2, allow this chapter to guide you into discovering your value. It's here to remind you that you're worth more than just ticking off tasks on a to-do list or getting through chores and work. Your time matters, and in these pages, you'll discover how to use it wisely, putting your energy where it counts most.

WHAT IS TIME BLINDNESS?

Have you ever felt as if time was almost speeding up? One minute, you're cleaning the kitchen to make breakfast, and then, before you know it, it's lunchtime. Well, it turns out that those of us with ADHD have quite a poor relationship with time, which is probably why you're always left feeling as if it's magically slipped out of your hands.

Time blindness is a sensory issue that occurs in people with ADHD; it makes it difficult for us to gauge the time and even sense it passing. If you have time blindness, you may have experienced the following symptoms:

- You often misjudge the time. You either completely overestimate or underestimate how much time has passed, how long the task should take, and how long you have remaining before starting your next task.
- You accidentally miss deadlines, events, and social gatherings because you can't gauge the time.
- Your schedules feel overwhelming and unrealistic as you have poorly estimated the required time.
- You always feel as if there is "not enough time in the day" or that you're "constantly losing track of time."
- You have a slow response or reaction time and often need a moment to process what's happening.
- You struggle to gauge how much time has passed since an event, which can make answering basic questions like "When did you have lunch?" or "When was your last vacation?" challenging.

Typically, your brain subconsciously counts your heartbeats so you can sense the duration of one minute. It also considers external factors, such as temperature and lighting. However, in an ADHD brain, this isn't the case.

As you may know, ADHD can make it difficult for us to complete tasks that are not enjoyable. Since waiting or timing is a neutral task, this may suggest that the ADHD brain is simply uninterested in gauging time. Research by Green (2023) also discovered that emotionally charged tasks increase our heart rate, which may play a part in disturbing our perception of time. Plus, our brain usually runs low on dopamine, a chemical that helps us regulate our emotions and behavior.

So, in simple terms, time blindness in ADHD could be caused by a combination of the brain not picking up on subtle cues that time is passing and not having enough of the right chemicals, like dopamine, to keep track of time effectively.

While it may seem that time blindness isn't a prevalent issue in your life, it can affect your work, friends, family, and even relationships. Missing deadlines and arriving late to the office is just the beginning of how time blindness manifests. Picture how many dates and special events you missed before. What about all the plans and promises you made to your partner that you couldn't fit into your day? Perhaps you've even rushed conversations and time with your loved ones to get back to completing late assignments and chores.

If you're anything like I was, you're tired of letting everyone down and being known as chronically late. You don't have to stay stuck in this negative loop—there's a way out, and we'll find the solution together.

MASTER TIME MANAGEMENT

If we want to say goodbye to time blindness, we'll need to say hello to time management. Think of time management as your new best friend; it will allow you to effectively organize and plan your time accordingly. And no, this doesn't involve simply dividing the hours of your day. Rather, it requires you to use various methods and tools that help you strategically tackle your day and harness the power of productivity.

We spend most of the day in an invisible tug-of-war with time. It's almost as if we're stuck in an alternate universe, begging to return to reality and reconnect with the present moment. While others can "see into the future" and gauge how close they are before a deadline must be met or chores have to be done, we're left mustering up motivation and questioning how much time we have left. Picture this as a ship slowly nearing the shore; a neurotypical individual would check in with the ship each day to see how close it is to reaching land. Whereas with an ADHD brain, it's almost as if your eyes are closed until the ship crashes into the sand, and you're frantically figuring out what to do. Sound familiar?

With time management, you'll learn the skills needed to successfully complete tasks on time. By implementing simple yet effective strategies, you will alleviate the unnecessary stress and fear that's weighing you down. You'll be able to finally escape the loop of "now" and take charge of your future. Let's see how it's done:

- **Maintain Habits and Routines:** Contrary to popular belief, ADHD brains work well with healthy habits and scheduled routines. Creating a realistic schedule that is easy to visualize and accomplish can boost your productivity and aid in time management. Make sure you start by implementing a simple schedule, such as a five-minute morning routine. Detail every task that needs to be done within five minutes, such as getting out of bed, making your bed, and brushing your teeth and hair. Then, use digital reminders like your phone and a big planner to help you stay on track. This is especially helpful for repeat offenders of the snooze button!

- **Take a Look at Time by Externalizing It:** Whether you have ADHD or not, you'll never know the exact time unless you have a clock. Externalizing time with clocks, to-do lists, and alarms may just be the gentle reminder you need to stay on track with your tasks. Consider investing in a clock for each room of your house. It may sound like a lot, but a simple clock from the dollar store may just save your day from disaster!
- **Practice Essentialism:** Essentialism is where you start the day by doing what you value the most. We know that our ADHD brains are motivated through excitement and passion, so why not tackle the task most important to you? For example, if you're planning to start a new business but still have to work your nine-to-five, kick off your day by taking thirty minutes to an hour to search brand names or business ideas. As long as you stay on track with your other tasks, this will help you achieve your goals.
- **Break Tasks into Chunks:** It's no secret that big tasks can feel overwhelming; breaking them down into bite-sized chunks will help alleviate some of that pressure. Take your task and divide it into three mini-tasks. Then, divide those mini-tasks into even smaller ones. This way, you'll be able to easily tick off each task as you complete it and stick to a designated time frame.

- **Set Reminders:** Investing in a big, visible calendar is a great start to remembering all the tasks you need to complete. However, setting the alarm to reinforce allotted time frames will help you go the extra mile to achieve your tasks. Each day, check in with your to-do list and set as many alarms for breaks and work hours as needed.
- **Analyze Patterns:** We're the first to call ourselves lazy or unproductive when it comes to failing to get a task done. However, chances are something was distracting you or taking your attention away from the task at hand. The next time you find yourself entering a negative space and beating yourself up for not being productive, retrace your steps and see what went wrong. Did you take enough breaks and eat enough food? Were you surrounded by noise or mess? Could you have taken a different approach to completing your work? By analyzing patterns, you can remove the self-inflicted blame and improve your time management skills!
- **Organize Your Things So You Won't Forget Anything:** There's nothing worse than sticking to a morning routine only to find yourself stuck with a million and one dirty plates and dishes and an overflowing trash can when it's time to make breakfast. Time management requires you to have the essentials in place. This means designating a place for your keys, wallet, jacket, and shoes. You should ensure you have a clean coffee cup and dish ready for the morning rush and that your laptop and phone are charged for work.
- **Ensure Your Task List Is Updated Weekly:** We live in a fast-paced society, so we must keep up, even with mundane tasks. Each week, sit down with your task list and evaluate your progress. Create different lists for household chores and work assignments; if you're

struggling with either list, you can consider approaching it from a different angle or reaching out to your partner or colleague for a helping hand.
- **Give Yourself Buffer Time:** We often underestimate the time it takes to complete a task, so allowing ourselves some buffer time is essential. You can do this by estimating the time you will take to complete specific tasks and then double it. For instance, if you think you can make a PowerPoint within an hour, allow yourself two hours for good measure. This way, you'll have plenty of time to complete all your tasks and avoid missing important details and stress.

Remember, you have everything you need within you to succeed. Simply take a moment to breathe, reconnect with the present moment, and apply the strategies you need to achieve your goals. You've got this!

PRIORITIZATION

Prioritization is a process that involves ranking a list of items in order of importance. It sounds easy enough, right? So, why do our ADHD brains find it so difficult to do?

If you have ADHD, chances are you've sat down to complete an assignment before and ended up spending hours of your day accomplishing nothing. You sit at your desk with a nice cup of steaming coffee, your laptop is charged, and your to-do list is detailed with everything you need to get done. Unfortunately, your brain and body didn't get the memo, and you're now stuck on a loop of scrolling Instagram, daydreaming, and questioning why you just can't stay focused. Once you've finally exited this negative cycle, you welcome feelings of dread and overwhelm as you pile up your list of tasks on tomorrow's to-do list. This is a story that's way too familiar for anyone with ADHD.

As much as you'd like to blame yourself for your poor prioritization skills, you should actually be pointing the blame at three symptoms of your ADHD:

1. **Time Myopia:** As we previously learned, our ADHD brains have a hard time looking into the future and planning ahead. We can't feel a sense of urgency until we can visualize the event happening a day, three days, or a week ahead of us. Hence, prioritizing our tasks can feel almost impossible.
2. **Big Picture Brain:** While creativity is a superpower, it can sometimes get a little out of hand. We can create beautiful big pictures with detail in our brains, even for solving issues. But, when it comes down to making decisions, we have so much in our minds that we can't figure out the most important or which possibility should be prioritized.
3. **Love of All Things Shiny and New**: We know that our ADHD brains thrive from excitement and emotion, especially when something new and shiny comes into the picture. So, when something excites you, whether it's a shiny Ferrari or a new work project, you're more tempted to jump ship and say goodbye to the old. However, not taking into account importance, relevance, and time can create a catalyst of issues in our to-do lists.

I know your current strategies and methods for approaching work, tasks, and chores are simply not working for you. You could be getting the best out of your day, spending more time with your partner, and reaching your goals, but you're trapped in a repetitive pattern and desperate to escape. Fortunately, with a few simple mindset shifts, you can change the narrative and live life to its fullest potential. Let's take a closer look:

- **You Can't Do It All**: You've convinced yourself that you are your Superman and that you can do it all. Whether it's work, kids, or household responsibilities, you're ready to do it all, even with a thumping headache, three missed deadlines, and sleep deprivation. I hate to be the bearer of bad news, but you simply cannot do it all. Believe me, I wish we could tackle everything on our own and finish the day with energy and enthusiasm, but we mostly end up feeling drained and exhausted. Prioritizing is essential to your mental and physical well-being; the sooner you realize this, the better you will feel.
- **Spending Time Gives You Time:** When we're stressed and overwhelmed, we tend to tackle any task we can just to get it over and done with. However, this often results in poorly done tasks, details missed, and mistakes made. We must shift the "go, go, go" mentality to "Let's take a moment and breathe." Once you've acknowledged that the world isn't ending and your tasks will get done, you can begin to prioritize them. This will allow you to approach them calmly and reasonably while avoiding unneeded anxiety and stress. While it may seem silly, spending time prioritizing will save you time in the future!
- **The Fact That It's Hard Makes It That Much More Important:** I can't be the only one who delays the hardest task until the end of the day, hoping that they're too tired or busy to complete it. After all, why would I put my competence and capabilities to the test? Unfortunately, this mindset doesn't achieve anything; we must instill self-belief and act confidently to reach our goals. Even if we fail

at completing the challenging task, we get back up, learn, and keep pushing forward until we are successful. Then, we will achieve a blissful sense of "I can do anything!"

Your only limit is yourself. Implement these three simple shifts, and within a matter of weeks, you'll achieve the highest sense of accomplishment.

TO-DO LIST

To-do lists are essential for staying on track with projects, assignments, household chores, and even social events. It's as simple as writing down the task and keeping it within a visible spot so you don't forget. Below, you will find two templates to kick-start your journey toward enhanced time management and task prioritization. Good luck!

To-Do List with Deadlines

Are you tired of missing deadlines and feeling that dreaded sinking feeling of "Oh no, not again!"? This to-do list has you covered; you'll be able to check in each day on a multitude of tasks and keep track of their progress.

Task	Date of Deadline	In Progress	Done	Discarded

"To..." List

It's time to get to the nitty gritty and jot down all of the important details about your project. This to-do list has been designed to keep track of information you simply cannot forget!

Task	Emails and/or Contacts	Specific Details	Date of Deadline

JOURNALING FOR SELF-REFLECTION

To finish Part 1 of this transformative journey, let's end on a high note with five self-reflection prompts. Grab your journals, get comfy, and take your time. Remember, this moment is about you and you only—embrace it.

1. To break patterns that don't benefit me, I will…
2. I hold unique value, and my impact on this planet is significant because…
3. On days of positivity, I uplift and inspire those around me by…
4. I've progressed from yesterday, as I am…
5. I spend too much time thinking about…

PART II
TOGETHER IN THE FAST LANE–BUILD A THRIVING RELATIONSHIP

In Part 1, we spent a lot of time with ourselves, rediscovering who we are, connecting with our authenticity, and embracing self-love and acceptance. We've allowed ourselves to heal and learned how to harness the power of ADHD. Now, it's time for us to spread the love and build a thriving relationship. Your partner deserves just as much love, acceptance, and compassion as you do, so let's ask them to join us on this journey to peek through their lens and understand their perspective. Get ready to build a thriving relationship based on trust, value, and empathy!

LOOK THROUGH THEIR LENS

"I've learned that people will forget what you said, people will forget what you did, but people will never forget how you have made them feel."

— MAYA ANGELOU

Have you ever wondered what life was like through your partner's eyes? Well, you're about to find out. ADHD can present many challenges for both you and your partner. Let's take a closer look and see how these hurdles may affect your relationship!

EFFECTS ON THE PARTNER WITH ADHD

If your partner doesn't have ADHD, you fear they might never understand you, at least not entirely. You're constantly nagged at, controlled, and micromanaged; sometimes, you question if they think you're a child and have regressed a decade or two. "Ugh, why can't they just get off my back?" is a thought that circles your mind at least once a week. No matter what you do, nothing is ever enough for your partner. You're trying your hardest to do your absolute best while managing a mind that runs a million miles an hour, but somehow, they just can't see that. You wish you could reconnect with the person you fell in love with, the fun, spontaneous partner who didn't care about responsibilities or household chores.

EFFECTS ON THE PARTNER WITHOUT ADHD

Being in a relationship with someone who has ADHD can create a lot of uncertainty and confusing feelings. You probably feel tired of taking care of someone else; you feel alone in your struggles and unappreciated for all your efforts. I'm sure there are times when you don't want to be the responsible or organized one anymore; you want to let go, be a slob, and have your partner pick up the slack for once. They make promises and swear to keep their word, but they never do when it comes down to it. You're forced to play the "bad cop" role and live a life of constantly reminding them what chores, events, and tasks they have to attend to. On top of that, you feel ignored, your needs aren't met, and sometimes you question if your partner cares at all.

HOW ADHD AFFECTS SEX AND INTIMACY IN A RELATIONSHIP

ADHD can have a bigger effect on sex and intimacy than most people realize. According to research conducted by Johnson (2021), a significant number of partners without ADHD felt as if their partners with ADHD preferred rough, fast, and often painful sex. Some individuals also reported that foreplay was often skipped, and their partners with ADHD jumped straight to intercourse. Researchers believe that this may be due to hyperactivity in ADHD. Impulses and a surge of energy may make slow and intimate intercourse appear slow, boring, or unsatisfying.

It's important to note that intimacy issues can be fixed; there truly is a solution to everything. With healthy communication, relaxation techniques, and even medication, you and your partner can discover what works best for you both!

THE PERKS OF DATING SOMEONE WITH ADHD

If you're dating someone with ADHD, you'll know just how incredible they are. Seriously, imagine dating someone who can wake up each day ready to tackle whatever adversity, challenges, and symptoms they're faced with. There is immense beauty, creativity, and passion hidden behind the symptoms of ADHD, some of which you may not have even noticed before. Let's wave goodbye to negative bias and welcome in the perks of ADHD:

- **Spontaneity:** Chances are, if you packed a suitcase right now and said "let's go" to your partner, they wouldn't even question running away with you on an adventure. While someone with ADHD may struggle to make plans and remember the details, they're the first ones to jump at new and exciting opportunities. People with ADHD make the perfect partners in crime; they're ready to do anything at the drop of a hat and are even prepared to face situations typically feared or perceived as scary. They truly understand the essence of living life to the fullest!
- **Sociability and Fun:** How many times have you dreaded a social gathering, family reunion, or event, and it turned out to actually be really fun? I bet your partner was with

you, too, weren't they? A beautiful aspect of ADHD is the energy that it brings to the table. Not only are people with ADHD ready to speak their thoughts and opinions to everyone in the room, but they're excited about it, too. They live their life with the level of confidence and radiance that many wish to have. In fact, it's almost contagious, as if being in their presence alone is enough to fill your body with energy and enthusiasm for the entire night.

- **Warmth and Love:** No one knows adversity better than someone with ADHD. Not only do people continuously discredit their condition, mock their symptoms, and put them down, but they also do it to their face. Just imagine how horrible it would feel to be in their shoes. Thankfully, people with ADHD don't take this negativity on board; they carry themselves with warmth, acceptance, and love. They know what it feels like to be judged unfairly and criticized for being who they are. Hence, they wouldn't dare do it to someone else, especially not their partner!
- **Encouragement to Try New Things:** ADHD pushes both you and your partner to step outside your comfort zone. A partner with ADHD allows you to view life through a different lens and encourages you to seek out adventures, which can deepen your connection and elevate quality time. No matter the adventure, your partner with ADHD is by your side, ready to keep the relationship interesting.
- **Open-Mindedness:** Have you ever had an outlandish idea? Maybe it was an idea that broke traditional standards and barriers. You probably thought that others would think it was "stupid" or "crazy" and feared their response to it. With a partner with ADHD by your side, you never have to worry that your thoughts, opinions, and ideas won't be valued. Their mind works in a unique way, so they're used

to feeling "different" than everyone else around them. They're ready to step outside of the box, and having a loving partner by their side makes it ten times more special!

- **Unique Perspectives:** People with ADHD are jacks of all trades and masters of none, making conversations and adventures much more fun. By now, they've hyper-focused on hobbies and interests a million times, so they're jumping at the idea of trying anything new. Want to get into arts and crafts, take up jiujitsu, or start baking classes? Your partner with ADHD is there for the ride, even if it only lasts a week!
- **Empathy and Understanding:** If you've had a rough day and just feel like jumping on the sofa and binge-eating your favorite snacks, trust me, you'll want your partner with ADHD there. Hard days are the norm for someone with an ADHD brain. They fall behind on assignments, get back on track, accidentally miss something important, and end up reorganizing the cupboards when they were supposed to take out the trash. So, they know exactly what it's like to have their day not go to plan. Whether you need an empathetic ear, an understanding perspective, or a shoulder to cry on, your partner with ADHD has got your back.

THE CHALLENGES OF THE OTHER PARTNER

It wouldn't be fair if we didn't take into account the effect ADHD has on you as their partner. As much as we'd like to gloss over the symptoms of ADHD and pretend they don't have a secondary effect on you, this simply isn't realistic. As their partner, you connect with them on an intimate level; you're with them every day through the ups and downs of life. It's not easy. Life can be confusing, especially when ADHD is thrown into the mix, so let's take a closer look at some of the emotions you may be feeling and gain some much-needed clarity:

- **Anger:** The dreaded cleaning duty—a constant battle between who has more chores. Whether you have ADHD or not, household responsibilities can be a bit of a romance killer. Finding out your partner forgot to load the dishwasher, take out the trash, or even make the bed can spark anger within us, especially if we have to constantly remind them. However, when your partner has ADHD, it can almost feel as if you are obliged to take the full load. You can see they've had a bad day, are overwhelmed, and are falling behind on their tasks, making it almost impossible to remind them of the list of chores they have yet to complete. So, like the kind person you are, you proceed to do their chores for them while bottling up your frustration and slowly resenting them. While chores can seem small and insignificant, sometimes, the small things tip us over the edge.
- **Exhaustion:** If your partner has ADHD, you may have slipped into a parent-child dynamic without even realizing it. As the non-ADHD partner, you are typically perceived as the more reliable, stable, and organized one. Hence, most of the responsibilities, chores, and special events or dates fall onto your shoulders. Now, you're left thinking for yourself and your partner, almost as if you were their parent. You have to remind them of important events they can't miss, ensure they are on track with work and finances, and check that they've done their fair share of household chores while maintaining a healthy lifestyle. This dynamic is uncomfortable for you and your partner;

they're tired of constantly being "controlled" while you're exhausted from nagging them all day.
- **Frustration:** "Ugh, why can't you just keep your promises for once and follow through with what you say?" This is a sentence many of us have thought or said a few too many times when our partners have missed an anniversary or failed to follow through with their words. Frustration can arise at any point in our lives; however, when our partners can't follow simple instructions, remember an important date, or keep a promise, it can feel hurtful. Even their poor time management and mess can be frustrating; being late to work because they lost the car keys or struggling to find a pair of matching socks because they were stuck in a doom pile on the kitchen table is frustrating!
- **Lack of Attention:** Having a conversation with your partner with ADHD can sometimes feel as if you're speaking with a brick wall. While our partners mean the best, and it's not entirely their fault, much of what we say goes in one ear and out the other. We could have a bad day at work, come home, and tell our partner, but nothing we've said has been acknowledged because they're hyper-focused on a task. Not only were our words ignored, but so were our feelings, making it hard to open up and trust that our partner genuinely cared for us.
- **Hurt Feelings:** Arguments, stressful days, and misunderstandings are common occurrences in life; however, for someone with ADHD, these situations can cause emotional outbursts. You are your partner's go-to person; you're the first person they see when they wake up and last before they go to sleep. Inevitably, you're going to take the brunt of their emotional blow-ups. In these moments, their behavior can be rude, hurtful, and

dismissive, causing our feelings to get damaged and offended.
- **Stress:** While impulsivity and spontaneity can be exciting, they can be stressful in the wrong situation. Whether your partner tells you they want to move to a new state, plan a quick trip to a country on the opposite side of the world, or quit their job, it usually involves some kind of financial risk. This can be extremely stressful if you have financial goals, low income, or simply aren't in a situation to spend money. Having contradicting dreams and goals can distance you from your partner and paint you as the "bad guy."

Every relationship experiences its highs and lows, but it's crucial that both partners feel loved and appreciated. Your needs deserve attention, your voice deserves to be heard, and you deserve to feel valued.

JOURNALING FOR SELF-REFLECTION

In Part 2, we will be switching up our approach to reflection time, so grab your journals, pens, and your partner for this activity. It's completely up to you and your partner to decide how you prefer to work on these questions. Some may enjoy reflecting as a team, whereas others may prefer spending their own time jotting down some ideas and merging together at the end to share thoughts and opinions.

Bear in mind that journaling requires a safe and comfortable space for it to be done effectively. Judgment, negativity, and shame should be completely avoided. If your partner wishes to share their reflections with you, acknowledge and accept them with positivity and love.

Prompts for the Partner with ADHD

1. What qualities do you love and admire the most about your partner?
2. Name five things you love about your home with your partner.
3. If you could have another superpower, what would it be?
4. What three things have made you smile this week?
5. Write a short love letter to yourself.

Prompts for the Partner without ADHD

1. What qualities do you love and admire the most about your partner?
2. What is something that has positively impacted your life this week?
3. What brings you joy?
4. What's your favorite way to spend your day?
5. Write a short love letter to yourself.

BUILD BRIDGES OF COMMUNICATION

"Ultimately the bond of all companionship, whether in marriage or in friendship, is conversation."

— OSCAR WILDE

Communication connects us all, whether it's friends, family, partners, or even a stranger on the street. Our words create memories and moments that stick with us for life. Maybe it was that time you chatted away with your partner, lost in conversation, sharing stories while holding a hot cup of coffee. Perhaps it was a sweet compliment and peck on the cheek as they said goodbye before work. Chances are, you could pinpoint countless memories of beautiful conversations that fueled your heart with love and mind with joy. Let's reconnect with the art of healthy communication to unlock a thriving relationship.

COMMUNICATION CHALLENGES

Every relationship has its fair share of ups and downs. However, when symptoms of ADHD are thrown into the mix, it's no longer just an argument between two people but also a battle with your partner's symptoms of ADHD. Impulsivity, inattentiveness, and hyperactivity can all impact your relationships to some degree; the real issue is how these symptoms affect your partner's communication skills. Picture healthy communication as the foundation of a thriving relationship. As time passes and each disagreement is left unsolved, your foundation begins to crack. Before you know it, you both feel disrespected, hurt, misunderstood, and unimportant. I'm not sure about you, but I wouldn't say that these emotions lead to a healthy and successful relationship.

With this being said, let's take a closer look at how poor communication skills may be affecting your relationship:

- **Interrupting:** Everyone has been interrupted before by a boss, colleague, or even a friend. However, you don't expect your partner to be the number one culprit. There is a high probability that your partner with ADHD cuts you off mid-sentence or interrupts you in nearly every conversation. While your partner may interrupt you without realizing it, it doesn't prevent those negative emotions from stirring inside you. It can make you feel like you've been ignored and misunderstood.
- **Dominating Conversations:** Don't you hate it when you're mentally processing one topic while the other person has already jumped to the next? Unfortunately, this is a common theme in people with ADHD. Their brains are running a million miles an hour, thinking of all the possible outcomes, situations, and topics that need to be

discussed. As a result, they dump all of their thoughts and ideas on the table, leaving you to feel as if the conversation has been dominated and that your perspective isn't valued. Keep in mind this isn't your partner's fault; an ADHD brain can't filter out unhelpful information like a neurotypical mind. An essential component of healthy communication is adequate space and time for each partner to address their own concerns.

- **Repeatedly Asking, "Are You Listening to Me?":** Your partner with ADHD can offer you intense focus and concentration in moments of hyperfocus. So, they expect you to offer them undivided attention in return, which is why they may ask, "Are you listening to me?" repeatedly. This can feel frustrating and annoying for you as a partner without ADHD, as you are listening and trying your best with the situation.
- **Struggling with Commitment Issues:** Before jumping to any conclusions, you should remind yourself that commitment issues don't mean your partner is unfaithful. As we know, ADHD causes a lot of trouble when it comes to focusing and paying attention. You may have noticed your partner getting lost in their own little world as your words go in one ear and out the other. Consequently, you may feel as if your partner isn't committed to the relationship. Perhaps you've wondered if they're taking the relationship seriously. This can cause a lot of uncertainty and anxiety within the relationship.
- **Exhibiting Rejection Sensitive Dysphoria**: Listen, those with ADHD have been severely criticized and rejected from social circles, jobs, relationships, and pretty much any situation you can think of. Hence, your partner may be highly sensitive if they fear your feedback on a disagreement is a personal attack. Certain things you may

say to your partner can feel like you're rubbing salt in a wound.
- **Experiencing Misunderstandings**: So, you're living with your partner with ADHD, you've witnessed their symptoms of ADHD firsthand, and you've seen one or two Instagram reels on the topic—you'd think you're a pro at ADHD by now, right? Sorry to break it to you, but there is so much more to ADHD than what you see on the surface. It's similar to an onion: You peel back one layer, and there are another ten to go. Your partner probably has a bunch of triggers and symptoms you may be unaware of and casually label as "annoying." They might even be causing continuous misunderstandings!

If you thought all hope was lost, you'd be wrong! Keep reading, and you'll uncover simple yet effective solutions to communication challenges.

IMPROVE COMMUNICATION

Think of healthy communication as a skill you must learn, almost like when you're in school and look forward to finally reaching that shiny diploma. With good communication, both you and your partner will possess all the tools necessary to build a trusting and strong relationship. Investing time into upgrading your communication skills won't just feel good but will also ensure that the pair of you feel seen and heard. After all, isn't that what we all want?

You'll finally be able to leave the past where it belongs and look forward to the future with a solution-oriented approach. You'll no longer fear those heated arguments that ruin your week or grow with resentment from snarky comments and passive aggression.

You'll be able to sit down with your partner and calmly approach the situation at hand with love and acceptance.

Honesty will become the best policy in your relationship. With good communication skills, you have to be prepared for total openness and authenticity. You will be truthful about your feelings and needs, create healthy boundaries in the process, and connect on an emotionally intimate level.

As stress and misunderstanding become a thing of the past, you will work as a team to take proactive steps toward building a beautiful future. I'm not sure about you, but I couldn't possibly miss out on the chance to improve my communication skills. However, before we jump into groundbreaking strategies for maintaining a healthy relationship, we need to take a few steps back and look at the causes of communication difficulties:

- **Neurological Factors:** Do you ever feel your words don't make any sense? This is because ADHD is linked with differences in brain structure and functioning. Your brain may struggle to pay attention, control impulses, and effectively communicate as it's not functioning at its best ability. Hence, your words can get a bit muddled at times, causing misunderstandings in your relationship.
- **Executive Functions:** If we think back to Part 1, we remember that people with ADHD struggle with executive function. This means that planning, organization, and emotional regulation can feel practically impossible. According to Sounderic (2023), research has found that these deficits can cause issues when it comes to communicating effectively, as they impact language processing.

- **Working Memory Deficits:** Working memory is the ability to retain information while using it, like while reading a book or having a conversation. As we discovered in Part 1, those of us with ADHD have impairments in working memory. This may make it difficult for you to follow along with what's being said in a disagreement and hard for you to express your thoughts and opinions successfully.
- **Impulsivity:** Many of us with ADHD will experience instant regret after saying something we probably shouldn't have. A common symptom of ADHD is impulsivity, which makes it difficult for us to think before we speak and can majorly impact our relationships. Perhaps we said something inappropriate, awkward, or even triggering for our partner.
- **Emotional Dysregulation:** ADHD involves big emotions that are often super hard to control, meaning our frustration, anxiety, and impatience are heightened in disagreements. This can make it challenging for us to get our point across successfully.

Tips for Improving Communication with ADHD

Having ADHD doesn't mean you're confined to a life of poor communication skills. With the right strategies and a bit of practice, you can face any conversation with confidence, clarity, and focus. Below are a few ways for you to improve your communication skills. Good luck!

- **Communicate Face-to-Face When Possible:** This may be a bit tricky for any long-distance couple, but having a face-to-face conversation makes a world of difference when it comes to disagreements. Communicating is already difficult, but when you opt for texting instead of talking, it is virtually impossible to understand the emotion and significance behind your partner's words. Plus, you can't read their body language or pick up on subtle cues telling you how they're feeling. If you can, always choose to talk about a disagreement face-to-face!

- **Prepare to Manage Distractions:** Our thoughts alone can be distracting; it's no secret that our mind runs a million miles an hour. This is why we must be prepared to manage them and redirect our focus to the conversation. If you know you have an opinion or ideas you want to voice but can't quite get a hold of, take a break from the conversation, step back, and tend to your needs. Try fueling your body with water and a snack, and proceed to jot down a few ideas. This way, you can present them calmly to your partner.

- **Acknowledge You Think Faster than People Talk:** Your ADHD brain is incredible; seriously, it thinks faster than your partner can even talk! However, this may cause you to blurt out the first thing that comes to your mind and cut your partner's sentence off. Undoubtedly, this is going to hurt their feelings. Instead of reacting to your impulses, try to redirect your focus to the present moment. Consider your body language, maintain eye contact, and ask simple questions to further understand your partner's thoughts and feelings.

- **Seek First to Understand:** Active listening involves listening with your ears, eyes, and heart to understand what your partner means beyond their words. Understanding will require you to listen rather than talk, see rather than judge, and open your heart with acceptance and love. Many of us are quick to listen to our impulses above everything and anyone else, but this time, you will have to push that urge down. I'm not saying it will be easy, but it will benefit your relationship. If you fear you'll forget an idea or opinion, simply write it down and revisit it once your partner has gotten a few things off their chest.

Tips for Improving Communication without ADHD

Just because you don't have ADHD doesn't mean your communication skills are perfect. It's time for you to polish those skills as a partner without ADHD and learn the art of effective communication. Here are my top tips and tricks for you to try out:

- **Acceptance:** Listen, your partner knows firsthand how difficult it is to have ADHD, and chances are they're frustrated with themselves, too. The key is to accept your differences and work together as a team to build healthy communication. No one is saying it will be easy, but it will definitely be worth it.
- **Don't Take It Personally:** This is probably one of the best lessons to implement when you live with someone with ADHD. Most of the time, they haven't thought through what they said and instantly regret it. Their ADHD is practically begging them to give in to urges and impulses, which include blurting out random pieces of information, ideas, and opinions that pop into their head. At the end of the day, it's best to forgive and forget.
- **Focus on Feelings:** You'll need to focus on your own feelings as much as your partner's. Emotions like frustration, agitation, and anger take a disagreement from calm to heated. This is something you want to avoid as it will cause big emotions and reactions from both sides of the relationship. Learning your triggers is the best way to deal with these tricky feelings. Perhaps there is a certain

word or boundary your partner may cross too frequently; think it through and talk with your partner.
- **Ponder Your Role:** Being neurotypical doesn't make you a saint, nor does neurodivergence make you a villain. Blaming everything on ADHD would be easy, but it's simply not true or fair. Whether you have ADHD or not, everyone is human and makes mistakes. It's important to remember that your relationship is a team; it takes two people to argue, two people to find a solution, and two people to create a thriving relationship.

As you work together to implement these strategies, your communication skills truly will blossom. Before you know it, you'll both become pros at healthy communication!

NAVIGATE CONFLICTS

Argument after argument, you and your partner tend to end up in a continuous cycle; one storms off while the other shuts down and goes mute. However, when ADHD is brought into play, conflicts can result in certain behavioral patterns that neurotypical couples may not experience. Disagreements can evolve into more than just storming off in frustration; they can also result in repetitive cycles and unhealthy dynamics. Let's take a closer look and watch out for patterns that resonate with your relationship:

- **Parent-Child Dynamic:** No one likes being micromanaged by their partner, nor does anyone enjoy constantly reminding someone to follow through with routines and chores. However, a relationship with ADHD can easily fall into this pattern. Usually, this is because one partner carries a heavier load of household chores, responsibilities, and tasks than the other. Perhaps the partner with ADHD struggles with remembering dates, keeping track of cleaning, and managing the family, so the partner without ADHD takes most of the responsibility. While this may seem like a harmless dynamic, resentment can slowly build on either side of the relationship. One partner behaves like a nagging parent, while the other feels like a naughty child. Clearly, this isn't a healthy dynamic for a relationship!

- **Chore Wars:** Chores are a common ground for disagreements in every relationship. Even if you have a schedule plastered on the wall from the first day of moving in together, slip-ups are bound to occur. However, as we saw in the parent-child dynamic, the partner without ADHD usually takes more responsibility for household chores than the other. The partner with ADHD is already stressed, struggling with managing their own tasks, and easily distracted, so the partner without ADHD concludes that they could complete all of the chores in less time and with less fuss. While this may be true, it is still an unfair distribution that will lead to resentment.

- **The Blame Game:** Do you ever feel as if your ADHD is the reason for every issue your relationship has? Well, this is probably because you are both playing the blame game. You and your partner may be blaming the tiniest of issues on ADHD when, in reality, they were simple human mistakes. Not only does this ignore the issue at hand, but it can also lead to the partner with ADHD feeling personally attacked and that their ADHD is to their detriment.

Fortunately, your relationship doesn't have to consist of heated arguments and unhealthy dynamics any longer. You can implement many excellent strategies as a team and work on building a thriving relationship. Let's take a closer look at the best ways for you and your partner to handle conflict:

- **Practice Mirroring:** Mirroring is an excellent practice that can be used in all areas of your life. Simply repeating what your partner has shared with you in an accepting manner will allow you room to further understand what they have said. Plus, it will acknowledge your partner's feelings. For example, imagine your partner said, "I feel like you don't put in as much effort as me with the household chores." You would mirror them by responding with, "I understand that you feel I don't contribute as much to household chores as you do. How about we talk it through to find a better balance?"
- **Be Direct about Important Issues:** Sometimes, our conflicts are more serious than imbalanced chore lists. This is why getting straight to the point with concise wording is often better than overtalking with emotion and insults. For instance, picture you're having financial issues. Instead of blaming the other by saying, "You recklessly spent our money like always, and now we have nothing!" aim for a more gentle and effective approach such as "We don't have the money to cover our electricity bill this month. We need to come up with a plan together." Don't forget to follow up with the mirroring technique to ensure your partner understands.
- **Use "I" Statements:** We want to avoid the blame game at all costs, which means swapping out "you" for "I." For example, imagine you're frustrated with your partner and say, "You never keep your promises." Instead, say, "I feel hurt when promises aren't kept." Simply reframing your statement will reduce the emotional damage on either side.

- **Grow in Understanding:** It's easy for us to blurt out our opinions and remain consistent with how we feel. I know I'm not the only one who stood by their "I'm right, and you're wrong" mentality in a heated argument. However, this doesn't get us anywhere, and it definitely doesn't build a thriving relationship. It's time for both you and your partner to drop selfishness and pick up empathy. Whether or not you agree with your partner, their feelings, thoughts, and opinions are valid. You should hear them out, accept them, and work on finding a solution rather than digging up the past.
- **Use the STAR Method:** The star method stands for "stop, think, act, and recover," which is a brilliant technique if you and your partner often find yourself getting quick to anger and easily frustrated.

    - **Stop:** When you notice your anger rising or big emotions coming to the surface, call for a break, such as "I think we should all take a moment to calm down." Then, go on a walk, listen to some music, or have a bite to eat. Make a pre-planned activity for moments when you need to take a break.
    - **Think:** Once you've both calmed down, regroup and discuss the issue at hand with logic and fact-based arguments. Remember, you want to keep those big emotions relaxed and avoid the blame game; taking a solution-oriented approach is the best way forward.
    - **Act:** Now, take the steps necessary to implement the solution you have both agreed upon.
    - **Recover:** As much as we'd all like to return to those lovey-dovey feelings after an argument, this just isn't realistic. You will both need time and

space to heal from the disagreement and process what happened. Be kind, empathetic, and loving as you take a day or two to get back to a healthy place.

JOURNALING FOR CONFLICT RESOLUTION

Whether you're a pro at communicating or not, conflicts will occur. Every healthy relationship has a disagreement now and then; the important thing is that you both understand how to deal with it successfully. So, the next time an argument arises and has somehow gotten a bit too out of hand, take a moment to step back and relax. Both of you can complete the ten journaling prompts below and jot down your ideas, opinions, and beliefs in your own time and space. Then, when you're ready, regroup and find harmony. Remember, there is an opportunity for growth, love, and acceptance in every argument.

1. What roles do I play in this conflict?
2. How can I gain a deeper understanding of my partner's viewpoint?
3. What potential resolutions exist for this conflict?
4. What outcomes do I anticipate for resolving this conflict?
5. In what ways has this conflict impacted our relationship?
6. Which behavioral patterns have contributed to this conflict?
7. How can my partner and I enhance our communication regarding this issue?
8. What might happen if we don't resolve this conflict?
9. What compromises are feasible for both my partner and me?
10. Have we overlooked any underlying issues that may have led to this conflict?

FIND BALANCE TOGETHER

"Next to love, balance is the most important thing."

— JOHN WOODEN

Love and commitment are not about sacrificing your beliefs or dismantling every boundary you've set. Instead, they're about balancing your values and nurturing your connection. In this chapter, we'll discover how your relationship can blossom with harmony and authenticity, guiding you toward a relationship where both partners thrive while staying true to themselves.

SHARE RESPONSIBILITIES

Do you remember that feeling of achievement when you were a child and cleaned your bedroom, put up a few posters, and moved a cabinet or two? You were so excited to show anyone and everyone what you'd just done. Well, this feeling sticks around even when you're an adult.

We spend hours of our day wiping, sanitizing, organizing, and vacuuming, hoping that someone appreciates our effort. I can't be the only one who's imagined their partner opening the door after a busy day at work and looking around the house in awe of everything I've done. Maybe even a hug and a "Wow, the house looks amazing, thank you! How did you do it all?" would be nice. After all, the idea that your home would become more welcoming and comfortable and offer a sense of love to your family is what makes cleaning, chores, and all of those mundane household activities worth it. But the reality is that there is no gratitude or appreciation for anyone who completes the chores. Instead, there's a constant battle about who does more than the other: the dreaded chore wars.

As we know, the partner without ADHD is typically left with the majority of the household responsibilities. The partner without ADHD will always be perceived as more organized, responsible, and stable in comparison to the partner with ADHD, who is stressed, chaotic, and forgetful. Hence, it only makes sense that the "more responsible one" takes the brunt of the work, whether it's paying the bills on time, taking the trash out every night, or giving the house its weekly clean. But what's the issue with this? It leads to exhaustion, resentment, and an imbalance.

ADHD doesn't mean you can't do chores, but it does imply that you must be strategic. Like anything in life, household responsibilities can feel overwhelming, so it's time to sit down with your partner and follow a three-step process to ending the chore wars for good!

Step One: Write the Rulebook

The first step to waving goodbye to the chore wars is establishing everything that needs to get done in the house. Grab a pen and paper and begin listing every single chore and household task that has to be done and how often. Does the bed need to be made every day? Do the floors need vacuuming twice a week? Do the windows need wiping every ten days? Create a realistic bullet-point list of what your house requires and what essential jobs are for you and your partner.

Step Two: Delegate

Now that we know what needs to be done, we can begin sharing the responsibility. Remember, the chores must be distributed equally so no one feels like they're putting in more effort than the other. This means that instead of just randomly dishing out each chore, you will need to consider the following points:

- **Desire:** Washing a stack of dirty dishes fills me with dread, but to my husband, it's a huge win if he's getting a warm, tasty meal each night. As you take your first pass over the list of chores, consider which chores you like the most or at least don't despise.
- **Ability:** Now, you'll need to consider your capabilities. There's no point signing yourself up to pay the bills each month and take care of taxes if you suck at finances. Be honest with yourself and decide what chores are within your scope of abilities.
- **Outsource:** If there are chores left on your list that neither of you enjoys, consider outsourcing them. Perhaps a monthly visit from a gardener is less stressful for you and your partner.

- **Time:** Lastly, you'll need to consider how much time you have in your day. If you commute to work, you'll probably be too tired to make dinner at night. If you have an early start, walking the dog may not be ideal for you. Consider how much time each task will take and if you can complete it within that time frame.

Once you've created your own master lists, take a moment to step back and evaluate each. Do they look manageable and fair? If so, well done! If not, you'll need to work together to figure out how each list can become more doable. Perhaps you need to outsource more than you had planned or even ask a friend or family member for help.

Step Three: Make a Chart

The last step involves making a scheduled chart. You will need to make time for each task in your chore chart and use it as a daily reminder of your responsibilities and obligations. Remember that you and your partner should have your own chart, and once completed, place it in a visible spot, such as the kitchen. This way, you'll be able to visualize each task that needs to be completed.

While this may appear simple, months of resentment and resistance to chores may cause a few hiccups. Think about it—household responsibilities play a huge role in arguments and disagreements in ADHD relationships. It's a topic usually surrounded by judgment, hurt, and frustration. So, when it comes to creating the list, the partner without ADHD may feel as if it's almost worthless, and the partner with ADHD will resume their normal antics. The partner with ADHD may feel overwhelmed or mistrusted. The key is to be patient with each other, allow the past to stay where it belongs, and make room for a solution-oriented mindset.

To help you and your partner effectively share responsibilities, consider applying the following tips and tricks:

- **Focus on Teamwork:** Chores will no longer be imbalanced, so it's time to ditch that "me" mentality and consider your relationship as a team. To create a healthy balance in the relationship, you and your partner will need to work together and rely on open and honest communication. This will mean regularly reviewing your chore charts as a team, checking in with each other, and asking how their chores went.
- **Resist Gender Dynamics:** Just because you're a woman doesn't mean you enjoy cooking, nor does being a man imply that you're great at dealing with bills and taxes. The last thing we want to do is assign chores simply because they're expected from us. You should assess the list while considering your interests and abilities.
- **Rotate the Drudgery Jobs If Boredom Becomes an Issue:** You may enjoy washing the dishes now, but it may be a completely different case in a month. Chores are boring, so why not switch them up now and then to avoid falling out of routine? You could consider creating a chore wheel and spinning it once a week to mix up your chore charts!
- **Gather Data, Not Resentment:** This is a completely new approach to tackling chores and responsibilities, so it's okay if it doesn't go to plan. You may take on more chores than you can handle or not have enough time in the week to complete them. That's okay! The key is to be patient and work with your partner to create a system that works for both of you. Imagine the first couple of days as a trial

run—see how it goes, gather data, and reevaluate at the end of the week. You can make adjustments where necessary.

Confronting the chore wars can feel like a lot to deal with at once, but trust me, when you've nailed a routine and found the perfect balance, you'll both wonder why you argued over it in the first place.

COMMUNICATE AND ESTABLISH BOUNDARIES

Whether it's with friends, family, partners, or even colleagues, everyone has boundaries—that invisible line no one should cross. Relationship boundaries help establish what is okay and not okay within your partnership. Typically, we create these boundaries to protect our mental or physical well-being. For instance, a physical boundary may be spending 20 to 30 minutes alone after work to destress and relax in your own space. An emotional boundary may be handling conflict without the use of insults or anger. Boundaries exist in all shapes and sizes, from emotional and physical to sexual and intellectual. They allow our relationships to build a sense of safety, trust, and respect.

It's important that you and your partner can clearly distinguish between healthy and unhealthy boundaries. An unhealthy boundary is either too rigid or too weak. A rigid boundary is often put in place to push others away, even family, friends, and partners. The individual may refuse to talk about their emotions or create time for loved ones simply because "it's a boundary." In contrast, there are weak boundaries where saying "no" feels virtually impossible, resulting in them taking more than the person is willing to give. An example of this is taking on too many responsibilities in a relationship.

Many of us in relationships have broken a boundary before out of love. Our partner may have needed extra help around the house, couldn't hold back their anger, or was just in a bad space, so we allow that invisible line to be crossed. While it may have felt like a caring thing to do at the moment, it creates the perfect foundation for toxicity, internal conflict, and resentment. Not only will you leave the situation feeling disempowered and hurt, but you will also suppress negative emotions. Inevitably, your mental well-being, internal peace, and relationship will suffer tremendously.

To create a healthy and happy relationship, boundaries are a fundamental component, so let's take a closer look at the four "C"s of boundary-setting:

1. **Clear:** We don't often discuss our boundaries, so when the topic pops up, we tend to shy away and lack confidence. This can cause confusion and even lead to the boundary being mistakenly broken. When talking to your partner about your boundaries, you will need to ensure you're using clear and concise language. You should spend time discussing it and going into detail to avoid having to repeat the conversation at a later date.
2. **Communicated:** As much as we'd like to be mind readers, we aren't. When setting your boundaries, you will need to be straightforward with your ideas and opinions. Implying something won't necessarily mean that your partner has understood it or even placed any importance on it. Hence, it's best to set boundaries before the conversation and write down the best way to explain it.
3. **Consistent:** Your boundaries must be fair and apply consistently to everyone else. Asking for 30 minutes of "me-time" after work but then spending it with friends, family, and everyone but your partner would just be cruel.

If your boundary doesn't apply to everyone equally, you can't expect it to be respected.
4. **Confirmed:** Once you've discussed your boundaries, your partner will need to confirm that they've understood it. Try referring back to Chapter 7, where you practiced active listening; this is the ideal time to implement it!

Boundary Setting for the Partner with ADHD

Your experience with ADHD might have led you to question whether setting boundaries is possible or even necessary, especially when your symptoms may create chaos around you. However, it's important to recognize that you deserve just as many boundaries as anyone else, regardless of your challenges. Let's take a closer look at how we can set healthy boundaries:

- **Understand That You Will Likely Need to Do Some "Work" to Enforce Your Boundaries:** Boundaries are one of those things that must be worked on daily to enforce. Your partner won't wake up one day and magically remember that you want 15 minutes of alone time before talking. It will take time, practice, and hard work to set them in place and create harmony between the both of you. The key is to be patient and allow the hiccups to happen without getting too caught up.
- **Start Small:** If you have a big list of boundaries, it's best to start small, or you might even forget them yourself. Take it step by step and slowly implement each boundary as you feel ready. Perhaps start with the most important one, such as a self-care night twice a week.
- **Choose Realistic Boundaries:** Creating realistic boundaries is essential if you plan to implement them successfully in

your daily life. Anything too far-fetched, such as eliminating all distractions from your environment at all times, regardless of the circumstances, simply just won't work.

Boundary Setting for the Partner without ADHD

Just because your partner has ADHD doesn't mean you can't have boundaries within your relationship. If you want to discover how to create and set boundaries on your own terms, try following the tips and tricks below:

- **Understand Your Boundaries:** Before discussing your boundaries with your partner, you should make sure you understand them first. Consider looking at your boundary from a different perspective and asking yourself some questions your partner may have for you. This way, you'll be well prepared and ensure it's conveyed clearly and concisely.
- **Learn to Say No:** While you may think your partner can't handle a "no" after a stressful day, they're as tough as nails. Seriously, your partner is stronger than you think, so give them the benefit of the doubt and stand firm by your boundaries. Just remember to be respectful, kind, and accepting of your partner.
- **Point Out Things That Make You Uncomfortable:** ADHD doesn't exempt your partner from the rules or lessen the damage that hurtful words or disrespect can cause. If a boundary is broken, make sure that your partner is aware of it. Now, I'm not saying this should lead to an argument, but reminding them that what they've done has crossed the line will avoid feelings of resentment and internal conflict.

MAINTAIN INDIVIDUALITY

You haven't seen your friends in months; hobbies and personal interests are a thing of the past, and all of a sudden, "me" and "I" have become "we" and "us." Then, that eerie thought creeps in: "Who am I?"

In a committed relationship, it could be easy to lose your individuality. At first, you're so excited to fall in love that you're swept off your feet and totally immersed in the experience of affection. You start doing everything together, from your favorite activities to waking up and eating breakfast. Gradually, time passes, and life without your partner almost becomes unimaginable. Don't get me wrong—attachment and codependence can be a beautiful sign of love and commitment, but they can also be detrimental to your well-being. Take a look at the signs below and see if you identify with the symptoms of losing your sense of self:

- **Your Well-Being Takes a Back Seat:** No one wants to see their partner upset, especially if there's anything we can do to prevent it. However, when we prioritize our partner's needs over our own, our emotional and physical well-being take the hit. You may lose sight of healthy eating habits, exercise, and even sleep.
- **You Sacrifice Your Happiness:** Every relationship requires sacrifice to some extent, whether moving cities for your partner's job or ditching the chips you wanted for your partner's favorite. However, these sacrifices should never be to your detriment. If you frequently brush off your own dreams, desires, and needs, it's time to take a closer look at your imbalanced partnership.

- **You're Afraid to Speak Up:** Many of us have feared that our partner may leave us if we speak up and voice our opinions. This inauthentic behavior causes us to represent a version of ourselves that isn't true to our beliefs and avoid rejection at all costs.

When you're in harmony with yourself, your needs, and your emotions, your relationship will blossom more than you could ever imagine. Allowing your authenticity to shine through will create space for a deeper connection and acceptance within your relationship. Here's how you and your partner can rediscover and maintain your individuality while in a relationship:

- **Realize What's Holding You Back:** Rediscovering your individuality may require digging deeper than you'd like. The majority of what's holding us back comes from a place of insecurity and fear. Perhaps trauma prevents you from speaking up as you fear your partner will walk out on you like your ex. Maybe it's a conditioned notion you were brought up with, such as your mom catering to your father's every need while abandoning her own. Whatever it is, try to pinpoint it!
- **Have a Heart-to-Heart with Your Partner:** Connecting with your individuality doesn't mean you and your partner have to call it quits, but it may require a little heart-to-heart. Discussing with your partner what you've been feeling and how you've neglected your own needs will allow your partner to understand your fears and insecurities better. In turn, they'll become more aware of their actions as you build yourself back up into the strong, independent person you've always been!

- **Dedicate More Time to Self-Discovery:** It's time to rewind the clock and revisit some of those hobbies and activities you used to enjoy. Whether it's self-care, movies, art, or exercise, discovering what brings you fulfillment will deepen your search for self-discovery.

Take it step by step, and before you know it, you will have created a beautiful, loving relationship that allows the pair of you to thrive independently!

JOURNALING TO CREATE HEALTHY BOUNDARIES

Healthy boundaries don't magically appear; they require hard work and dedication. So, grab your journals, pens, and partners to spend some time working toward a beautiful future by answering the following questions:

1. What do you find challenging to refuse? What might happen if you said no?
2. Identify your top three values. Then, suggest one action for each to honor those values.
3. Recall a time when you felt disrespected. Describe the communication before, during, and after the incident.
4. If you were drafting rules for your relationships, what would be the first five?
5. What are your non-negotiables in a romantic relationship?
6. Do you have a personal motto? How have you recently exemplified it? If you don't have one, what would it be, and how would you embody it?
7. Name something you wish you did more consistently. What's preventing you from doing it?
8. What behavior do you wish to decrease? What strategies can you employ to reduce it?

9. When was the last time you received a negative response? How did it unfold, and what did you learn?
10. List ten actions you'd ideally accomplish in a week. Commit to completing at least one weekly.

INTIMATE LEVELS OF CONNECTION

"True love is not a hide-and-seek game: in true love, both lovers seek each other."

— MICHAEL BASSEY JOHNSON

As we come to the end of our journey, it's time for us to forget the guessing games, misunderstandings, and arguments that once clouded our love and affection. Let's focus on today, tomorrow, and the future as you discover emotional and physical harmony with your partner.

EMOTIONAL INTIMACY

Do you know that feeling when you first meet someone and are desperate to get to know them more? You wish you had a window into their mind and could see their deepest desires and thoughts. We yearn to know more, connect with them, and become a part of their lives. That is emotional intimacy, and it goes far beyond physical connection and sex; it's where two people's thoughts, feelings, wins, struggles, and life experiences delicately intertwine.

Allowing someone to see your true self in your most authentic form is where emotional intimacy grows. You let your guard down and open your heart and mind to your partner. In return, you gain a profound sense of trust in them and a connection so strong it could build a lifetime of love and partnership. Keep in mind that emotional intimacy can appear differently in everyone. For some, it involves feeling safe and able to share your deepest secrets, dreams, and ambitions without fear of judgment. For others, emotional intimacy is when their partner takes a genuine interest in their feelings and day-to-day experiences; they travel with them through the ups and downs of life.

Either way, the benefits are the same: a profound sense of trust and security. Emotional intimacy allows you and your partner to always have a home within each other, a place to go when the days get rough, and a partner to celebrate with when life rewards you. You don't fear vulnerability but embrace it, creating a connection that supports your dreams, hopes, and goals. I know it almost sounds too good to be true!

- **Be Strategically Vulnerable to Earn Their Trust:** Mixing "strategy" and "vulnerability" in the same sentence can feel a little counterproductive, but trust me, if you want to break down your partner's guard, this is the way to go. Even when we've been in a long-term committed relationship with someone, it can still be tricky to let down our emotional wall. As their partner, you obviously want them to confide in you and show their vulnerability, so you must take the first step. Try sharing past experiences and emotions with your partner that were difficult for you to manage. Over time, your partner's guard will slowly crack until they're ready to be vulnerable with you.

- **Give Your Partner Daily Affirmations and Compliments:** Regardless of how long you and your partner have been together, you should always appreciate their positive attributes. Regularly complimenting your partner confirms your love and care for them. It will make them feel special and seen, something that we all deserve to feel. You don't even have to make it into a huge moment; it can be simple, such as "I want you to know how much I love you" or "I really appreciate the time you take to listen to me."
- **Prioritize Sexual Satisfaction:** According to a study conducted by Yoo et al. (2013), couples who felt that their sexual needs were met experienced greater emotional connection. While sex isn't the answer to all of your relationship troubles, taking the time to learn and explore both your sexual needs and desires may improve your emotional connection and strengthen your bond.
- **Make an Effort to Break Out of Your Day-to-Day Routine:** While it's only natural, life can get pretty boring when you stick to your mundane comfort zone. You and your partner should spend more time together than just dinner and bedtime. Consider breaking your routine and spicing things up with a cute date night, watching a movie at the cinema, or attempting a fun dance class together. Breaking from your routine isn't something that needs to be planned, either. For example, if you've eaten dinner and crave a sweet treat, make it a little adventure and take a stroll to an ice cream parlor or grab some baking ingredients.

The trick is to have fun, share a few laughs, get to know each other better, and turn off autopilot. Life is about thriving, not just surviving!

PHYSICAL INTIMACY AND ADHD

One of the blessings of ADHD is that it allows us to find excitement in so many elements of life, from new activities and hobbies to romantic relationships and exploring our sexuality. However, you may have noticed that this excitement doesn't always last. Your hobby eventually loses its wow factor, and you're eager to find the next exciting thing. Well, this same pattern of behavior can occur in our sex lives.

Initially, you're just getting to know your partner and exploring your intimacy with them; it's new, fun, and satisfying. As time passes, your physical intimacy slowly becomes less and less passionate. While this is only natural, it doesn't prevent that feeling of boredom from kicking in. Now, I'm not saying that this issue arises in every relationship with ADHD, but a recent statistic suggests that more than 40% of women and men with ADHD have sexual difficulties (Pagán, 2022).

If sexual boredom isn't a feeling that resonates with you, your ADHD may be affecting your intimate life in one of the following ways:

- **Trouble Paying Attention during Intimacy:** We often think that poor focus only applies to work, chores, and mundane activities, but it can also interfere with your sex life. If you find your mind wandering during sex and thinking of things that don't apply to the current situation, your partner may notice and feel like you're not interested

in them. Plus, it will also make it more difficult for you to feel satisfied.
- **High or Low Libido:** Some people with ADHD experience a high sex drive, leading them to consistently watch pornography and experience sexual urges. On the other hand, some people experience a low sex drive as antidepressants and ADHD medication lower their libido. It's fifty-fifty as to which one you may or may not experience.
- **Emotional Irregularity:** If you think about it, emotional irregularity playing a part in our intimate lives makes total sense. Those of us with ADHD know that mood swings are common and hard to manage. This means that sexual urges and desires may pass or arise within a super short time span. You may also experience hypersensitivity, where sensations such as touch can feel too intense. You may enjoy a certain sexual act in one moment but find it overwhelming in the next, making healthy communication and boundaries incredibly important!

Keep in mind that ADHD can affect your sex life in a multitude of ways. What's important is that you and your partner can work together to find a sexually rewarding and satisfying relationship. Here are a few tips and tricks to get you started:

- **Have a Conversation with Your Partner:** Never underestimate the power of healthy communication. Try talking with your partner about your symptoms and how they affect your intimacy. It's essential that your partner understands it's not a sign of disinterest or a lack of love.
- **Remove Any Distractions from the Bedroom:** Your bedroom should be a comforting and relaxing place for you and your partner to unwind. Removing any mess or

reminders of your day-to-day stress will help you become more focused. Try replacing it with comfy blankets, pillows, candles, and relaxing dim lights.
- **Boost Intimacy through Physical Touch:** Simple touches such as hand-holding, kisses, hugs, and rubbing your partner's feet after a long day can help boost intimacy and enhance your relationship. Physical touch shouldn't be a one-in-a-while deal but a simple daily expression of your affection, care, and love for each other.
- **Consider Talk Therapy:** If you believe your symptoms of ADHD are majorly affecting your intimacy, therapy is the best option. You can work with a professional alongside your partner to learn skills and strategies to improve your relationship.

With the right strategies in place, healthy communication, and a bit of fun, you and your partner don't have to become part of a statistic where ADHD ruins your intimacy. Instead, you can create your own path to a thriving relationship filled with understanding, connection, and love.

JOURNALING FOR SELF-REFLECTION

As we end our final chapter, work with your partner on these ten journaling prompts for self-reflection. Just because our journey toward creating a thriving relationship has to come to an end doesn't mean that your time spent on self-improvement and discovery is over.

1. Recall a significant life lesson that has shaped you. What was it, and how did it impact you?
2. Reflect on your transformation and evolution over the period you spent reading and implementing the strategies in this book. What changes have you noticed in yourself?
3. Revisit the happiest memory you have. Dive into the details: where were you, who were you with, and what made that moment so special?
4. Outline your priorities for the upcoming week, month, or year. Do these align with your long-term aspirations and goals?
5. Share a deeply personal secret, one you've never revealed before. What makes this secret so important to you?
6. Identify the individuals in your life who provide constant support and belief in you. What makes their encouragement so meaningful?
7. Select three photographs from different stages of your life. Describe the circumstances surrounding each picture and reflect on the person you were at that time.
8. Consider three relationship challenges you've faced and overcome. How have these experiences contributed to your resilience?
9. If given the chance, would you change anything about your life? Why or why not?
10. Reflect on the role of journaling in your life. How has it helped you grow, and have you noticed any changes in your relationships as a result?

BE AN INSPIRATION FOR SOMEONE ELSE!

ADHD is a part of your life, but it doesn't define you, and you can work with it to nurture a thriving relationship. If you remember how it felt when you weren't confident about this, why not take this opportunity to share hope with someone who's feeling lost right now?

Simply by sharing your honest opinion of this book and a little about your own experience, you'll help new readers find the guidance they need to make their ADHD an asset in their relationship.

Thank you so much for your support. May your life be filled with love and connection!

Scan the QR code below:

CONCLUSION

And just like that, you and your partner learned the art of teamwork while creating a thriving relationship. Doesn't it feel amazing? Has your communication improved? What about your connection? Are you closer than ever before? I bet you've also started a journey to discovering your individuality, right? I'm so excited to hear all about your and your partner's incredible transformation!

I'd be lying if I said this journey was easy. It took a lot of hard work, dedication, and commitment. You've accomplished something truly remarkable, and it all started in Part 1, where you began your journey to self-discovery. You unraveled the complexities of ADHD and fought stigma and criticism while breaking down myths and barriers. You learned the pillars of self-worth, effectively boosted your self-esteem, and waved goodbye to that inner critic. Now, you know how to manage your symptoms of ADHD while living life with confidence, resilience, and positivity. I bet it feels empowering, doesn't it?

Once you understood how your ADHD affects your daily life, you ventured into Part 2 with the help of your partner. There was a lot to unpack here, from getting to the root of arguments and misunderstandings to battling the chore wars and responsibilities. But you both came out stronger than ever, improving your communication skills, setting healthy boundaries, and even upgrading your emotional and physical connection. You two are equipped to face any challenge life throws your way. But, in the meantime, you'll be enjoying your thriving relationship!

Before we say goodbye, I want you to remember that ADHD doesn't define you; it's an endless source of empowerment and strength. Every day, wake up and work together as a team, choosing to better yourselves with healthy communication, honesty, and authenticity. Use the tools and strategies you learned to create a long-lasting, successful, and loving partnership—you deserve it!

Take it one step at a time, have patience, and savor every laugh, memory, and loving moment that life brings your way. When you need a helping hand, the pages of this book will be here to guide you.

Until then, I'll see you later, lovebirds.

REFERENCES

Ackerman, Courtney E. "What Is Self-Acceptance? 25 Exercises + Definition & Quotes," *PositivePsychology.com*, July 12, 2018, https://positivepsychology.com/self-acceptance/.

"ADHD & Time-Blindness." *Attention Deficit Disorder Association*, January 11, 2019, https://add.org/adhd-time-blindness/.

Allen, Susan. "Self-Love with ADHD: The Big Heart Approach," *Additudemag*, March 12, 2021, https://www.additudemag.com/self-love-adhd-acceptance/.

Ameer, Muslim. "How to Identify Your Personal Strengths and Weaknesses." *LinkedIn*, April 21, 2023. https://www.linkedin.com/pulse/how-identify-your-personal-strengths-weaknesses-muslim-ameer/.

Barkley, Russell. "Managing Adult ADHD: Impulse-Control Rules to Live By." *Additudemag*, August 20, 2021. https://www.additudemag.com/adhd-impulse-control-social-spending/.

Basso, John C., Alexandra McHale, Victoria Ende, Daniel J. Oberlin, and Wendy A. Suzuki. "Brief, Daily Meditation Enhances Attention, Memory, Mood, and Emotional Regulation in Non-Experienced Meditators." *Behavioural Brain Research* 356 (2019): 208–220. https://doi.org/10.1016/j.bbr.2018.08.023.

Berwid, Oliver G., and Jeffrey M. Halperin. "Emerging Support for a Role of Exercise in Attention-Deficit/Hyperactivity Disorder Intervention Planning." *Current Psychiatry Reports* 14, no. 5 (2012): 543–551. https://doi.org/10.1007/s11920-012-0297-4.

Brito, Jenna. "Dating Someone with ADHD: What Is It Like?" *Medical News Today*, August 3, 2023. https://www.medicalnewstoday.com/articles/dating-someone-with-adhd#positives.

Burnett, Marissa. "ADHD and Boundaries: The 4 Cs of Boundary Setting." *Unconventional Org*, February 23, 2023. https://www.unconventionalorganisation.com/post/adhd-and-boundaries-the-4-c-s-of-boundary-setting.

Caldwell, Michael. "3 Reasons Why Prioritizing Is So Hard with an ADHD Brain." *ADDept*, 2021. https://www.addept.org/living-with-adult-add-adhd/why-prioriitizing-is-hard-with-adhd.

Cherry, Kendra. "The Components and Psychological Study of Creativity." *Verywell Mind*, 2019. https://www.verywellmind.com/what-is-creativity-p2-3986725.

Cherry, Kendra. "11 Signs of Low Self-Esteem." *Verywell Mind*, February 13, 2023. https://www.verywellmind.com/signs-of-low-self-esteem-5185978.

Cherry, Kendra. "What Are the Benefits of Having ADHD?" *Verywell Mind*, December 12, 2023. https://www.verywellmind.com/adhd-benefits-advantages-challenges-and-tips-5199254.

"Clockify - Free To-Do List Templates." *Clockify*. https://clockify.me/to-do-list-templates.

"Control ADHD, Set Good Boundaries." *ImpactParents*, April 26, 2021. https://impactparents.com/blog/adhd/control-adhd/.

Cummins, Marla. "ADHD Adults Communicate Better Using These 7 Listening Tips." *Marla Cummins*, November 14, 2022. https://marlacummins.com/adhd-adults-and-challenges-listening/.

Dahl, Dan. "ADHD Quotes about the Neurodivergent Way of Paying Attention." *Everyday Power*, April 15, 2022. https://everydaypower.com/adhd-quotes/.

"Data and Statistics about ADHD." *Centers for Disease Control and Prevention*, August 9, 2022. https://www.cdc.gov/ncbddd/adhd/data.html.

Defontaine, Janine. "105 Writing Prompts for Self-Reflection and Self-Discovery." *Reflections from a Redhead*, November 19, 2019. https://reflectionsfromaredhead.com/writing-prompts-for-self-reflection/.

"Diagnosis of ADHD in Adults." *CHADD*. https://chadd.org/for-adults/diagnosis-of-adhd-in-adults/#:

Fagan, Jason. "Understanding ADHD Time Management: Tips and Tricks." *ATTN Center*, February 13, 2023. https://attncenter.nyc/understanding-adhd-time-management-tips-and-tricks/.

"Female vs Male ADHD." *The ADHD Centre*, December 21, 2022. https://www.adhdcentre.co.uk/female-vs-male-adhd/.

"5 Tips for Effective Communication with Your ADHD Partner." *Inner Compass Counseling & Coaching*, December 15, 2022. https://innercompasscounseling.com/5-tips-for-effective-communication-with-your-adhd-partner/.

"4 Ways to Keep Your Identity in a Relationship." *Psych Central*, June 14, 2017. https://psychcentral.com/health/why-men-give-up-their-identity-in-a-relationship#signs.

Gepp, Kylie. "ADHD Gender Differences: Signs, Diagnosis, and More." *Medical News Today*, October 31, 2022. https://www.medicalnewstoday.com/articles/is-adhd-more-common-in-males-or-females#diagnostic-criteria.

Gould, Wendy R. "4 Things You Can Do Right Now to Build Emotional Intimacy with Your Partner." *NBC News*, February 6, 2020. https://www.nbcnews.com/better/lifestyle/how-build-emotional-intimacy-your-partner-starting-tonight-ncna1129846.

Green, Robert. "ADHD Symptom Spotlight: Lack of Focus." *Verywell Mind*,

February 25, 2022. https://www.verywellmind.com/understanding-and-managing-lack-of-focus-in-adhd-5216984.

Green, Robert. "ADHD Symptom Spotlight: Time Blindness." *Verywell Mind*, May 11, 2023. https://www.verywellmind.com/causes-and-symptoms-of-time-blindness-in-adhd-5216523#:

Hall, Jenna. "18 Time Management Tips for People with ADHD." *Calendar*, December 16, 2022. https://www.calendar.com/blog/18-time-management-tips-for-people-with-adhd/.

Hallowell, Edward. "ADHD and Sexuality: When Distractions Ruin Romance." *Additudemag*, December 13, 2023. https://www.additudemag.com/learning-to-linger/#:

Holmquist, Jennifer. "ADHD and Marriage: How to Handle Common Conflict Patterns." *Focus on the Family*, August 26, 2022. https://www.focusonthefamily.com/marriage/adhd-and-marriage-how-to-handle-common-conflict-patterns/.

Hoogman, Martine, Janita Bralten, Derrek P. Hibar, Maarten Mennes, Martijn P. Zwiers, Lisanne S. J. Schweren, Kimberley J. E. van Hulzen, Sarah E. Medland, Ekaterina Shumskaya, Neda Jahanshad, Peter de Zeeuw, Eszter Szekely, Giovanni Sudre, Thomas Wolfers, Anne M. H. Onnink, Jeroen T. Dammers, J. C. Mostert, Yvonne Vives-Gilabert, Guido Kohls, and Erik Oberwelland. "Subcortical Brain Volume Differences in Participants with Attention Deficit Hyperactivity Disorder in Children and Adults: A Cross-Sectional Mega-Analysis." *The Lancet. Psychiatry* 4, no. 4 (2017): 310–319. https://doi.org/10.1016/S2215-0366(17)30049-4.

"How to Set Boundaries with Your Partner." *Verywell Mind*. https://www.verywellmind.com/how-to-set-boundaries-with-your-partner-6834034.

Hughes, Lisa. "4 Communication Problems in ADHD Relationships (and How to Fix Them)." *Get In Flow*, January 29, 2023. https://www.getinflow.io/post/fix-communication-problems-in-adhd-relationships.

"Improving Communication Skills with ADHD." *Modern Therapy*, June 6, 2019. https://moderntherapy.online/blog-2/improving-communication-skills-with-adhd.

Incledon, Natasha. "How Low Self-Esteem Affects Relationships." *Peacefulmind*, April 11, 2018. https://peacefulmind.com.au/2018/04/11/how-low-self-esteem-affects-relationships/.

Jacobsen, Jess. "10 Effects of Lack of Attention in Relationships & Remedies." *Marriage Advice - Expert Marriage Tips & Advice*, July 23, 2019. https://www.marriage.com/advice/relationship/lack-of-attention-in-relationship/#:

Johnson, Jamie. "What to Do When Your Partner Has ADHD: Coping, Treatment, and Healing." *Healthline*, May 20, 2021. https://www.healthline.com/health/

adhd/adhd-spouse-lonely#sex-and-intimacy.

Jones, Harper. "Can ADHD Cause Problems with Memory?" *Verywell Health*, October 1, 2023. https://www.verywellhealth.com/can-adhd-cause-memory-issues-5207991#:.

Klein, Allen. "Tips on How to Focus with ADHD." *Psych Central*, June 24, 2021. https://psychcentral.com/adhd/adhd-tips-to-fire-up-your-focus#tips.

Lee, Crystal I. "How to Regulate Emotions as an Adult with ADHD." *LA Concierge Psychologist*, October 18, 2021. https://laconciergepsychologist.com/blog/regulate-emotions-adult-adhd/.

Lisane. "Learn Better Boundaries and Build Better Relationships." *Shaping Freedom*, June 14, 2022. https://shapingfreedom.com/poor-boundaries-relationships/#:.

Lovering, Natalie. "ADHD Impulsivity Symptoms, Management, and Outlook." *Medical News Today*, May 22, 2023. https://www.medicalnewstoday.com/articles/adhd-impulsivity.

Low, Kendra. "Using Your Memory with ADD as a Therapeutic Strategy." *Verywell Mind*, December 6, 2023. https://www.verywellmind.com/add-and-working-memory-20796#:.

Manager, Carb. "10 Ways to Reframe Your Negative Self-Talk." *Carb Manager*, October 2023. https://www.carbmanager.com/article/zoevtbaaab8ahfu3/10-ways-to-reframe-your-negative-self-talk.

Mayo Clinic. "Adult Attention-Deficit/Hyperactivity Disorder (ADHD) - Diagnosis and Treatment." *Mayo Clinic*, January 25, 2023. https://www.mayoclinic.org/diseases-conditions/adult-adhd/diagnosis-treatment/drc-20350883.

Mind Tools Content Team. "What Is Time Management?" *Mind Tools*, 2022. https://www.mindtools.com/arb6j5a/what-is-time-management.

Morin, Amanda. "8 Common Myths about ADHD." *Understood*. https://www.understood.org/en/articles/common-myths-about-adhd.

Mowlem, Florence, Jessica Agnew-Blais, Eric Taylor, and Philip Asherson. "Do Different Factors Influence Whether Girls versus Boys Meet ADHD Diagnostic Criteria? Sex Differences among Children with High ADHD Symptoms." *Psychiatry Research* 272 (2019): 765–773. https://doi.org/10.1016/j.psychres.2018.12.128.

Murray, Aja L., Tom Booth, Michael Eisner, Bonnie Auyeung, Graeme Murray, and Denis Ribeaud. "Sex Differences in ADHD Trajectories across Childhood and Adolescence." *Developmental Science* 22, no. 1 (2018): e12721. https://doi.org/10.1111/desc.12721.

"Myths and Misunderstandings." *CHADD*, 2018. https://chadd.org/about-adhd/myths-and-misunderstandings/.

National Health Service. "Diagnosis - Attention Deficit Hyperactivity Disorder

(ADHD)." *NHS*, 2019. https://www.nhs.uk/conditions/attention-deficit-hyperactivity-disorder-adhd/diagnosis/.

National Health Service. "Treatment - Attention Deficit Hyperactivity Disorder (ADHD)." *NHS*, December 24, 2021. https://www.nhs.uk/conditions/attention-deficit-hyperactivity-disorder-adhd/treatment/.

National Health Service. "Types of Talking Therapy." *NHS*, February 17, 2022. https://www.nhs.uk/mental-health/talking-therapies-medicine-treatments/talking-therapies-and-counselling/types-of-talking-therapies/.

"Navigating Stress and ADHD: Tips to Reduce Triggers and Relieve Stress." *Attention Deficit Disorder Association*, November 10, 2023, https://add.org/stress-and-adhd/.

Nigg, Joel. "How ADHD Amplifies Emotions." *ADDitude*, February 15, 2018. https://www.additudemag.com/emotional-dysregulation-adhd-video/.

Pagán, Camille N. "ADHD: Is It to Blame for Your Sexual Issues?" *WebMD*, August 25, 2022. https://www.webmd.com/add-adhd/adhd-sexual-problems.

Parekh, Ranna. "What Is ADHD?" *American Psychiatric Association*, 2022. https://www.psychiatry.org/patients-families/adhd/what-is-adhd.

Pierce, Randi. "Poor Self-Image and ADHD: How to Improve the Way You See Yourself." *Life Skills Advocate*, November 25, 2022. https://lifeskillsadvocate.com/blog/poor-self-image-and-adhd-how-to-improve-the-way-you-see-yourself/.

Poissant, Helene, Aline Mendrek, Nicole Talbot, Bassam Khoury, and John Nolan. "Behavioral and Cognitive Impacts of Mindfulness-Based Interventions on Adults with Attention-Deficit Hyperactivity Disorder: A Systematic Review." *Behavioural Neurology* 2019 (2019): 1–16. https://doi.org/10.1155/2019/5682050.

Prasetyo, Fandy. "100 Journal Prompts for Self-Acceptance and Validation." *Lifengoal*, April 16, 2022. https://lifengoal.com/journal-prompts-for-self-acceptance/.

Rabinowitz, Lee. "13 ADHD Communication Styles That Create Conflict in Most Marriages." *Rabinowitz Counseling*, August 22, 2023. https://counselorforcouples.com/13-adhd-communication-styles-that-create-conflict-in-most-marriages/.

Raheja, A. D. D. "How Impulsive Behaviour Is Destroying Your Relationship." *Hope Care India*, June 12, 2021. https://hopecareindia.com/how-impulsive-behaviour-is-destroying-your-relationship/.

Reid, Samantha. "Setting Healthy Boundaries in Relationships." *Help Guide*, March 1, 2023. https://www.helpguide.org/articles/relationships-communication/setting-healthy-boundaries-in-relationships.htm.

Ripper, Janine. "23 Insightful Journal Prompts Perfect for Self-Reflection - with a

Free Printable!" *Reflections from a Redhead*, September 17, 2019. https://reflectionsfromaredhead.com/journal-prompts-self-reflection/.

Robinson, Kara Mayer. "What Is Your Non-ADHD Partner Thinking?" *WebMD*, April 24, 2019. https://www.webmd.com/add-adhd/features/what-non-adhd-partner-thinking.

Romanelli, Amy. "How Forgetting Can Damage a Relationship." *Psychology Today*, May 21, 2021. https://www.psychologytoday.com/intl/blog/the-other-side-relationships/202105/how-forgetting-can-damage-relationship.

Sachdev, Priya. "What Is Emotional Dysregulation?" *WebMD*, June 22, 2021. https://www.webmd.com/mental-health/what-is-emotional-dysregulation.

Saline, Sharon. "Conflict Resolution: A Skills Guide for ADHD Families and Relationships." *ADDitude*, March 13, 2023. https://www.additudemag.com/slideshows/conflict-resolution-skills-family-relationships-adhd/.

Schultz, Jane. "Stressors and the ADHD Brain: Pandemic Coping Advice." *ADDitude*, September 12, 2023. https://www.additudemag.com/stressors-adhd-brain/.

Scott, Elizabeth. "Quick and Simple 5-Minute Meditation for Stress Relief." *Verywell Mind*, September 22, 2022. https://www.verywellmind.com/practice-5-minute-meditation-3144714.

Scott, Elizabeth. "The Toxic Effects of Negative Self-Talk." *Verywell Mind*, November 22, 2023. https://www.verywellmind.com/negative-self-talk-and-how-it-affects-us-4161304.

Shrout, Ryan. "What Are the Effects of Stress on a Relationship?" *University of Nevada, Reno*, November 13, 2018. https://www.unr.edu/nevada-today/news/2018/atp-relationship-stress.

Silver, L. "The Neuroscience of the ADHD Brain." *ADDitude*, September 7, 2017. https://www.additudemag.com/neuroscience-of-adhd-brain/.

Sinfield, Jennifer. "How the ADHD Brain Biologically Differs from the Non-ADHD Brain." *Verywell Mind*, February 28, 2017. https://www.verywellmind.com/the-adhd-brain-4129396.

Smith, Melinda. "Adult ADHD and Relationships." *HelpGuide.org*, 2019. https://www.helpguide.org/articles/add-adhd/adult-adhd-attention-deficit-disorder-and-relationships.htm.

Sreenivas, Sushma. "ADHD in Women." *WebMD*, March 18, 2021. https://www.webmd.com/add-adhd/adhd-in-women.

Stavraki, Iro. "ADHD and Low Self-Esteem: Signs, Causes and Coping Mechanisms." *Simply Psychology*, October 25, 2023. https://www.simplypsychology.org/adhd-low-self-esteem.html.

Taft, Theresa. "ADHD Impulse Control: 5 Strategies to Tame Your Impulsive

Behavior." *Psych Central*, March 1, 2021. https://psychcentral.com/adhd/adhd-in-adults-5-tips-for-taming-impulsivity#mindfulness.

Tallon, Monique. "10 Simple Ways to Practice Mindfulness in Our Daily Life." *Monique Tallon*, April 13, 2020. https://moniquetallon.com/10-simple-ways-to-practice-mindfulness-in-our-daily-life/.

"10 Journal Prompts to Help You Set Healthy Boundaries." *Inside Then Out*, February 5, 2023. https://www.insidethenout.com/blogs/news/10-prompts-to-help-you-set-healthy-boundaries.

"3 Steps to End the ADHD Chore Wars for Good." *ADDept*. https://www.addept.org/add-adhd-marriage-relationship/stop-fighting-over-chores.

"The Benefits of Knowing Your Strengths Now, Rather Than Later." *Career & Professional Development Center | University of Utah*. https://careers.utah.edu/peaks-and-valleys/29/#:

"Understanding ADHD and Communication Difficulties in Adults." *Sounderic*, August 2, 2023. https://www.sounderic.com/post/understanding-adhd-and-communication-difficulties-in-adults.

Vanbuskirk, Sarah. "Why It's Important to Have High Self-Esteem." *Verywell Mind*, February 24, 2021. https://www.verywellmind.com/why-it-s-important-to-have-high-self-esteem-5094127.

Wade, Derek. "ADHD Time Management Tips and Suggestions." *Medical News Today*, June 2, 2023. https://www.medicalnewstoday.com/articles/adhd-time-management#improving-time-management.

Westcott, Kyrus. "10 Uplifting Quotes to Inspire Introverts with ADHD." LinkedIn. Last modified June 28, 2023. https://www.linkedin.com/pulse/10-uplifting-quotes-inspire-introverts-adhd-kyrus-keenan-westcott/.

"What I Love Most About You (and Your ADHD, Too)." *ADDitude*, February 9, 2018. https://www.additudemag.com/slideshows/loving-someone-with-adhd-positive-qualities/.

Williams, Grant. "How to Maintain Your Individuality While in a Relationship: 7 Tips." *Hily*, June 2, 2023. https://hily.com/blog/how-to-maintain-your-individuality-while-in-a-relationship/.

Wooden, John. "John Wooden Quote." *Goodreads*. https://www.goodreads.com/quotes/554454-next-to-love-balance-is-the-most-important-thing.

Yoo, Hyunhee, Suzanne Bartle-Haring, Randal D. Day, and Rashmi Gangamma. "Couple Communication, Emotional and Sexual Intimacy, and Relationship Satisfaction." *Journal of Sex & Marital Therapy* 40, no. 4 (2013): 275–293. https://doi.org/10.1080/0092623x.2012.751072.

Made in the USA
Middletown, DE
24 July 2024